Airborne

Charles MacDonald
Airborne

Editor-in-Chief: Barrie Pitt
Art Director: Peter Dunbar

Military Consultant: Sir Basil Liddell Hart
Picture Editor: Robert Hunt

Executive Editor: David Mason
Designer: Sarah Kingham
Special Drawings: John Batchelor
Cartographer: Richard Natkiel
Cover: Denis Piper
Research Assistant: Yvonne Marsh

Photographs for this book were especially selected from the following Archives: from left to right page 7 Imperial War Museum; 8 IWM; 10 Heinrich Hoffman; 11 Ullstein; 12-13 IWM; 14-15 US National Archives; 16-17 IWM; 18 US Army; 19 IWM; 20 IWM; 21 IWM; 22 US Army; 23 IWM; 28 Das Deutsche Museum; 30 US Army/IWM; 31 IWM; 32-33 IWM; 33 IWM; 34 IWM; 35 IWM; 36-37 IWM; 38-39 IWM; 40 Ullstein; 41 US Army; 42-43 IWM; 43 Ullstein; 44-45 IWM; 47 Suddeutscher Verlag; 50 IWM/Ullstein; 51 Ullstein; 54-55 US Army; 56 Bibliothek fur Zeitgeschiche; 60 IWM; 61 Sudd. Verlag; 62-63 IWM; 68-69 IWM; 70-71 IWM; 71-73 IWM; 74-75 IWM; 76-77 Sudd. Verlag; 78 Sudd. Verlag; 79 IWM; 80-81 IWM; 81 Associated Press; 82-83 Brown Brothers; 83 Sado Opera Mundi; 84-85 Sudd. Verlag; 86-87 Sado Opera Mundi; 90 Ullstein; 94 US Army/IWM; 95 IWM; 96 IWM; 96-97 IWM; 100 IWM; 104 US Army; 106-107 IWM; 108-109 US Army; 112-113 US Army; 114 US Army; 116-117 IWM; 118 US Army; 119 US Army; 120-121 IWM; 122 IWM; 124 IWM; 125 IWM; 127 Sado Opera Mundi; 128 IWM; 130-131 IWM; 132 IWM; 134-135 IWM; 136 IWM; 138-139 International News; 140-141 US Army; 142-143 US Army; 144 IWM; 146 IWM; 147 IWM; 149 IWM; 150-151 US Army; 152-153 US Army; 154 IWM; 156 IWM

First printing: May 1970
Printed in the United States of America

Ballantine Books Inc.
101 Fifth Avenue New York NY 10003

Contents

8   'Something in great style'

28   The outcome of Operation Market

56   The rise and fall of airborne forces

90   Early Allied developments

104   The path to D-Day

128   Towards a climax beyond the Rhine

154   Whither the airborne

160   Bibliography

Airborne Forces
Brigadier Anthony Farrar-Hockley DSO MBE MC

If a nation decides to prepare for war, there is much to be said for beginning with an empty armoury. A completely new range of war equipment is likely to be not only more mechanically efficient but ought also to lead to innovation in strategy and tactics. Germany found itself in this position to an extent when it began re-armament under Hitler's direction in the 1930s. Hence its success in the development of the tank and the dive-bomber. Hence the inception of airborne forces.

As with the tank, the Germans borrowed the idea of assaulting their enemy with troops from above. Yet unlike their imaginative and dynamic development of armoured warfare, they denied General Student, their airborne commander, the full support and facilities that his force deserved. The first nation seriously to employ the airborne assault, they did so hesitantly and in small numbers. When at last they disposed a mass of men and machines in order to capture Crete, the operation came near to failure owing as much to multiple commitment as to the errors of the defending allies. Yet Crete *was* taken by airborne assault – the Royal Navy denied access to the German seaborne force – and it was Student's constant regret that the losses of thirty per cent he incurred overshadowed the victory. Malta was due to be taken by much the same means, yet Hitler held back. Could Malta, weak in troops and without air or armoured strength, have survived an assault by three airborne corps in the spring or summer of 1942?

The Allies began late and with some doubts, yet rightly persevered in bringing eventually seven American and British airborne divisions into service. Unfortunately, few of the higher commanders understood the potential these forces offered. The parachute and glider operations in Normandy demonstrated, particularly on the left flank, their strategic and tactical capabilities. Notwithstanding several crass errors during planning, Operation Market Garden came close to permitting a full-scale crossing of the Rhine in the autumn of 1944 – perhaps to achieving what Field-Marshal Montgomery attempted: the outflanking of the German frontier defences. Fortunately, General Eisenhower was not discouraged by the losses of the 1st Airborne Division at Arnhem so that their Anglo-American colleagues were used in mass again and with success on the final Rhine-crossing and entry into the German heartland early in 1945.

It is fitting that Charles B MacDonald should have been chosen to write the account of Airborne Forces in this series of Ballantine Books. For he was not an airborne soldier but an infantry officer of no mean experience. He has thus appraised his subject without personal ties, yet with an understanding of battle conditions. This comprehension is enhanced by his wide knowledge of the war as a senior official military historian in Washington, and as the author of a number of exemplary studies of the Second World War. This book adds to his high reputation.

'Something in great style'

An early morning haze having cleared, Sunday 17th September 1944 had turned into a lazy, beautiful late summer day. Across the verdant flatlands of the Netherlands the Dutch faithful, dressed in the drab, ill-fitting clothes that went with four years of German occupation, made their way home from church or sat down to a Sunday dinner that was short on meat, long on potatoes. Here and there, at once a part of the crowd and yet isolated, strolled or bicycled German soldiers absorbing the sunshine and rest of a day away from their posts.

German commanders too, for the most part, took their ease. The catastrophic *hegira* from northern France and Belgium that had followed Allied landings in Normany appeared for the first time to be nearing an end, particularly in the north where the labyrinthian Dutch canals and the sprawling expanses of the Maas, Waal, and Neder Rijn (lower Rhine) rivers provided ready defense lines.

Near Amsterdam a Luftwaffe general who was Chief of the Occupation had gone with one of his staff for a leisurely dinner at a country restaurant. The *Polizeiführer*, chief of the Gestapo in the Netherlands, had departed his command post early to pass the day with German friends in The Hague. An SS battalion commander had left word with his adjutant that he was to be disturbed for no reason; he was spending the day in his quarters with his Javanese mistress.

Beneath the red-tiled roof of a commandeered Dutch country cottage a few miles south of the Maas river, *General der Fallschirmtruppen* Kurt Student, his tunic unbuttoned, sat at a desk in his bedroom, consumed with the paper work incidental to his profession. Head of a former training command, the First Parachute Army, that had hurried to the Netherlands only a fortnight before to fill a great gap in the German line, Student wanted to be near his tele-

9

phones, for there were some indications that the British had chosen that day for renewing their attack. On the other hand, the morning had developed fairly quietly. Even the buzzing and occasional strafing of Allied fighter planes that Student had noted and sometimes had followed with a practiced eye from the balcony of the cottage could be dismissed as little out of the ordinary for such a clear day.

In the park setting of Hotel Tafelberg, in a western suburb of Arnhem on the north bank of the Neder Rijn, *Generalfeldmarshall* Walter Model, commander of Army Group B – his monocle, as always, in place over his right eye – descended from his room to join senior members of his staff in pre-lunch aperitifs. As an orderly poured from a carafe, others put last minute touches to tables set up in the glass-enclosed portico of the hotel.

Like Student, Model half expected an early attack by the British, possibly even that day. It might develop, Model had decided, fairly close along the flank of the American First Army at Aachen, although a secondary effort might be made northward in the direction of Arnhem to peg the left flank on the Waal river ten miles south of Arnhem at Nijmegen. Yet since the morning had passed with little more than apparent nuisance raids by Allied aircraft, Model was prepared to relax a bit. Reports of a German counterattack that had begun during the morning against the Americans at Aachen encouraged relaxation. If the American thrust could be stopped, the entire Western Front might be stabilized in the concrete fortifications along the frontier, the Westwall, or – as the Allies called it – the Siegfried Line.

Like Student and Model, *SS-Obergruppenführer und General der Waffen SS* Willi Bittrich – a strikingly handsome man who once had tried a career as an actor – also spent the morning in his command post. There, twenty miles east of Arnhem, Bittrich was concerned less with possible British actions than with the complicated logistical moves of the two SS panzer divisions under his command. It had been not quite two weeks since Field-Marshal Model had ordered Bittrich

and headquarters of his II SS Panzer Corps to the Netherlands, there to supervise rebuilding of one of the severely depleted panzer units and moving of the other into Germany for more complete refitting.

Yet even as Bittrich had tried to bring some order out of incipient chaos, the high command in Berlin had changed the plan. One of the divisions, the new word had come, was to be shifted against the Americans at Aachen. General Bittrich in turn had decreed that this was to be the 10th SS Panzer Division, which had received the first replacement equipment to reach the corps: twenty-seven Mark V Panther tanks.

On the morning of 17th September the 10th SS Panzer Division's commander was on a brief leave in Germany, while his staff was preoccupied with the myriad details of getting the men ready for the move to Aachen. An advance guard of one reinforced battalion already had departed, but before the remainder could march, the division had to absorb relatively intact portions of the other panzer division, the one that was to fall back into Germany.

Because the commander of the second division, the 9th SS Panzer, had been wounded in the retreat from France, the officer in charge was the Chief of Staff, *Obersturmbannführer* Walter Harzer. That morning of the

Below: Field-Marshal Model, of Army Group B. *Right:* General Student of First Parachute Army

17th Harzer was in fine fettle. By having his men remove the guns from the division's remaining tanks and armoured cars, he had been able to report that the vehicles were disabled and thus could not be turned over to the 10th SS Panzer Division. He was particularly proud that in this manner he had saved almost intact his pet unit, the division reconnaissance battalion. That very morning Harzer was to motor to the battalion's assembly area to bestow a decoration on the commander.

A staff car in mid-morning transported Harzer to the edge of an airfield north of Arnhem where the battalion, 500 men strong, was drawn up for the ceremony. Wearing duelling scars on his left cheek as if they were a military decoration, Harzer took the salute. It was great, just like the old days of peace. The ceremony over, Harzer joined the battalion's officers for a convivial celebration in the officers' mess, set up in a bunker alongside the airfield.

Of all the German commanders behind the forward fighting line in the Netherlands, only one appeared to be in some measure unusually alert. That was a relatively junior officer, Major Sepp Krafft, commander of a depot battalion only recently formed, mainly from nineteen year olds with a liberal sprinkling of older men who had done their first marching in the Great War. The battalion was attached to the headquarters of the Chief of the Occupation. Two days before, Major Krafft had dined with the aging Chief of Staff, *Generalleutnant* Hans von Tettau.

'Something is turning up,' Tettau had said as the two officers lingered over a post-dinner glass of port and a cigar. 'Today over the whole *Reich* and England too we had the nicest weather, but in spite of this, not a single big bomber came.' The Allies, Tettau went on to explain, were at a critical point in the war. They could ill afford to let even one good day pass unused. 'It proves,' Tettau said, 'they are preparing something in great style.' Krafft wanted to know if the general had warned his superiors.

Aircraft for the Arnhem drop are drawn up on a British airfield

13

American C47s cross the calm North Sea

'They treated me like an old man,' Tettau said sadly. 'They only laughed at me.'

Returning to his billets at a country estate called Waldfriede, west of Arnhem, Sepp Krafft had found General von Tettau's words sticking like flypaper in his mind. Concerned about he knew not what, Krafft the next morning had ordered an outlook posted in a turret atop the big country house.

On Sunday, 17th September, as the haze cleared and the day grew bright, Major Krafft thought again of Tettau's warning. Late in the morning British planes bombed an objective in Arnhem, then American planes hit some objective not far from Waldfriede.

Was 'something in great style' about to occur? What was it? Were they going to try to seize the big airfield north of Arnhem? Already in recent weeks they had bombed it several times. Were they after the big Rhine bridge at Arnhem? Or was it something else? Or nothing at all?

As noon approached, Krafft grew increasingly nervous. He ordered all his men confined to quarters on full alert and brought out a ration of gin.

'Mark my words,' said one of the old German soldiers to the Dutchman who owned the estate; 'something is turning up. They always give us gin when important things have to be done.'

In mid-morning that Sunday, the air above south-eastern England whirred with a tremendous roar and drone as if a generation of locusts had developed motors and long-range wings. From twenty-two airfields, 1,545 C-47 troop-carrying aircraft and 479 thin-skinned gliders bearing men, vehicles, weapons, and equipment took to the air to rendezvous above the coastline and head eastward in two great streams. Another 1,000 fighter planes rose with them to weave a protective curtain about the big, slow-moving troop carriers.

Beginning the night before, almost 1,500 other British and American planes, including over 900 big B-17 Flying Fortress bombers, had already begun a campaign that was to become, as Hans von Tettau had predicted, 'something in great style'. Careful to spread their missions about lest a pattern be discernible, the planes bombed and strafed airfields and anti-aircraft gun positions in the general vicinity of Arnhem and other flak positions along the two routes the troop-carrying planes were to follow.

Within the C-47s and the gliders few of the men would admit to being afraid, even nervous. Yet the fact that most of them quickly began to doze, some to sleep soundly, even before the planes had crossed the cheerless waters of the North Sea, belied their efforts at composure. It is strange how men under tension succumb to sleep.

Two-thirds of the men were American, the other third British. One American, Sergeant Ross S Carter, a veteran of three other parachute jumps, saw the start of the flight this way: 'Seated in the planes like grim steel-trap-jawed automatons, all softness, smiles and good humour vanished from our faces, we waited for the newest episode to unfold . . . The armada of planes . . . circled and roared and then formed into long curving formations that darkened the sky for hundreds of miles . . . Most of us sat quietly and smoked cigarettes, trying as best we could to confine our reflections and mental images within the vacuum of nothingness.'

'The apprehension and concern of the veterans,' noted Brigadier-General James M Gavin, a wiry thirty-seven year old who commanded the 82nd US Airborne Division that was to drop south of Arnhem near Nijmegen, 'was no less than that of the recruits, but they seemed to show it less.' To veterans and newcomers alike, the flight was a new kind of experience, for never before had they participated in an airborne attack in daylight. Heretofore night had been the rule; but so plagued had night drops been by dispersion – the men scattered like chaff before the wind – that commanders had decided to risk the wrath of enemy anti-aircraft guns and jump by day.

Major Anthony Deane-Drummond, a British communications officer, marveled at how peaceful everything looked below his plane. 'The North Sea,' he recalled, '. . . for once was like a millpond with scarcely a ripple to disturb its brown-looking water.' The men in his plane, Deane-Drummond also noted, were 'nearly all asleep'.

The commander of the 1st British

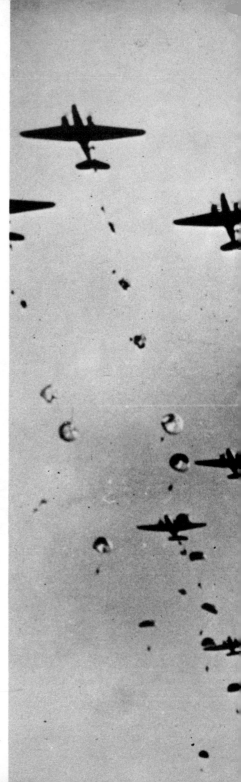

Airborne Division, scheduled to drop farthest north near Arnhem, was Major-General Roy E Urquhart, until this operation a ground commander given to air sickness whenever he flew. Urquhart rode in a glider in the northern column. 'I glanced ahead and below' – the general noted – 'where I could see four other tugs and their gliders and, on an uncommonly calm sea, the air-sea rescue craft stationed for our greater safety at comforting intervals . . . Presently when the tow-rope snapped between one tug and its glider, I saw air-sea rescue vessels moving smartly towards the ditched glider . . . and then we were over the coast of Holland.'

In a C-47 plane in the southern column, Major-General Maxwell D Taylor, commander of the 101st US Airborne Division, which was to drop farthest south, did like most of the men around him – he slept. He awakened once to eat a canned ration, then dozed off again.

Almost everybody had expected the enemy's flak to begin at the Dutch coast, but the Allied fighters and bombers that had come first had apparently done their job well. The planes in the northern column drew anti-aircraft fire only as they moved inland toward Arnhem and Nijmegen. Those in the southern column, flying over friendly Belgian territory en route to drop zones closest to the front lines, drew no fire until they swung across the ground fighting front. There a swell of flak and small-arms fire rose from German positions. Most of the fire fell short of the planes, but not all of it.

Plane 32, carrying men of the 101st Airborne Division, came in for a heavy share of the fire. Hardly had the plane passed the front lines when one shell rocked the craft perilously, then a second set the right motor afire. As gasoline sprayed along that side of the plane, flames spread with a rush, entering through the side and the floor. Not waiting for a green light to signal the jump, the paratroopers bailed out. The crew chief and radio operator followed. Two

The First Allied Airborne Army
Left: US paratroopers relax on the
way over. *Above:* Their British
counterparts also seem quite
unperturbed

men looked up to see their parachutes on fire. Not until they were
less than 300 feet from the ground
did their emergency 'chutes open.
Plane 32, its two pilots still inside,
circled for a moment, then glided to
the ground. It disappeared in a fury
of explosion and flame.

Occasional tragedy stalked the
planes carrying men of the 101st
Airborne Division all the way to the
drop zones north of the city of Eindhoven. In the same plane with General
Taylor, Lieutenant-Colonel Patrick
Cassidy, a battalion commander, saw
a plane carrying part of his regiment's
Company A burst into flame. He
counted seven men leaping from the
burning ship before it trailed out of
sight behind him. His own plane
rocked and bumped from explosions
all about it.

The red warning light was on and
the men were adjusting their gear

and hooking their static lines when
Cassidy saw flames break from a
plane just off the left wing. Neither
the crew nor the men inside appeared to know they were afire. Concerned with the fate of the blazing
ship, Cassidy failed to see the green
light when it flashed. 'Cassidy,' General Taylor said softly, 'the green light
is on.' 'Yes, sir,' Cassidy answered;
'I know it.' Still Cassidy hesitated,
until at last he saw the first figure
plunging from the neighbouring plane.
With that, he jumped.

The major portion of the men of the
101st made successful jumps, though
in a number of cases pilots of crippled
planes, holding doggedly to course,
were lost. Freak accidents, too,
occurred. Two men who got out of
their plane safely met death as a
crashing C-47, propellers whirling, cut
them to pieces. Another plummeting
plane careened into a group of men
who had already made it to the ground,
killing three.

As flak began to explode around
planes carrying men of the 82nd
Airborne Division in the northern
column, here is how Sergeant Carter

reacted: 'A shell rocked us. My God! To sit like clay pigeons at attention in the belly of our big-tailed bird and be shot at! I wanted to jump, to be on the ground. In the plane it was *take* and I wanted to *give*. I wanted out so bad that I would have jumped with a red-hot stove in my arms . . . Each second wound our nerves a little tighter. If we didn't jump soon, they'd uncoil and mess up like the spring in an overwound watch.

"Stand up and hook up!"

I was to be the last man out. If we were hit, I was sure to go down with the plane . . . The parachute, Tommy gun, eleven magazines of 45 ammo, anti-tank mine, hand grenades, sleeping bag, ration-filled musette bag, and other items gripped and strangled and oppressed. My breath came in short gasps. God! Would they never start jumping?

. . . The line began to shuffle up to the door. Everything fine. No more ack-ack . . . As I released my static line I turned to look at the crew chief standing teacup-eyed and hang-jawed in the tail of the plane. The whimsical reflection, "What in hell is he scared of? He's not gonna jump," accompanied me falling, turning, twisting, waiting and hoping into space. Then I felt the snap-up pull of the opening chute and looked up gratefully at the billowing green silk.'

To a platoon leader in the 82nd's 508th Parachute Infantry, First-Lieutenant Wayne H Smith, the flak on the skin of his plane sounded like hail falling on a tin roof. 'The twenty minute warning sounded. I woke those who had gone to sleep . . . Then four minutes before jump time, the red warning light flashed on. I stood in the doorway, inspecting my men . . . As the green light flashed on, almost at once a burst of flak appeared in front of the door. The man who was to jump first said, "It's sure hot; let's go!" And within the space of a few seconds, the plane was emptied.'

Everywhere the sky bloomed with parachutes, and the countryside floating up to the soldiers in their harness could have been in most

Left: The drop begins; troops and equipment. *Right:* The British gather their supplies

Above: **Major-General Maxwell D Taylor, commander of 101st Airborne Division.** *Right:* **The main objective, the highway bridge at Arnhem**

cases a parade ground in North Carolina, so peaceful did it seem. Some men incurred scratches and bruises as their parachutes failed to deflate quickly upon landing and the wind dragged them along; a few broke their legs; and one man landed on his side, the impact forcing the sight of his sub-machine gun through the flesh of his left leg. A big equipment bundle struck another on the head and killed him. Yet most men of the 82nd Airborne Division made it to earth much as they had done before in training jumps.

The most eventful departure from plan was the drop of First-Lieutenant John Thompson and his 'stick' of six men.

'When the green light came on,' Lieutenant Thompson recalled, 'I noticed we were directly over a group of buildings and decided to wait a few seconds and jump on a field just southwest of the bridge, which I could see plainly a short distance away. The remaining eight planes jumped on the prescribed signal . . . Then out we went!'

As Thompson and his men floated earthward, they became aware that they were coming down far from any of the other men, only a few scant yards from the south end of one of the three most important objectives assigned to the airborne troops, an imposing span carrying a highway over the Maas River near the town of Grave, south of Nijmegen. It was at once a disturbing yet challenging realization.

Farther north, one of the first

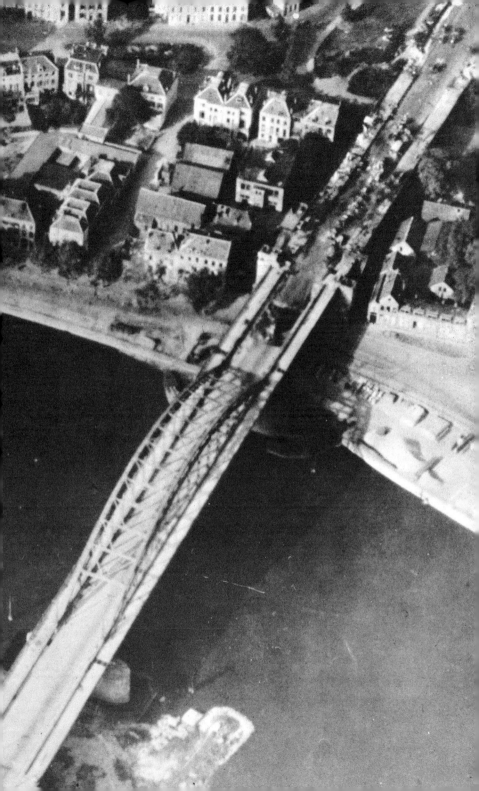

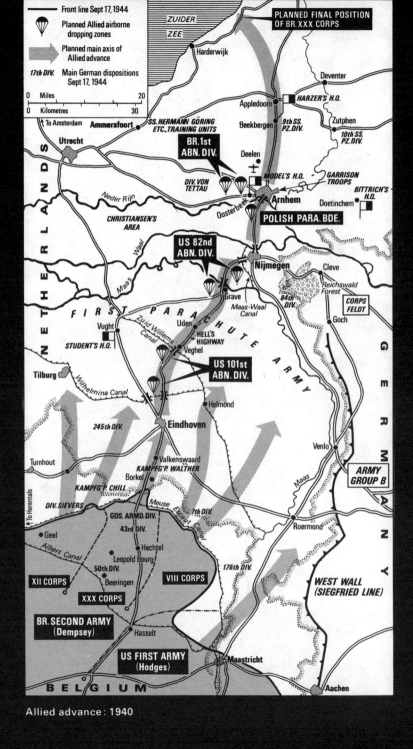

Allied advance: 1940

paratroopers to jump was Major B A Wilson, a veteran soldier whose nickname of 'Boy' belied an age of forty-five. Wilson was in charge of the pathfinders who were to mark the drop and landing zones west of Arnhem for British troops and gliders. As did most of his men, Boy Wilson believed the opposition would be weak, the attack short-lived. Against that possibility, he had packed a dress uniform in his parachutist's leg-bag, along with a bottle each of whiskey, gin, and sherry.

To Wilson and his pathfinders, the jump seemed at first like an exercise in Hampshire. The countryside was to all appearances peaceful. Great expanses of purple-blue heather contrasted sharply with the green of woods and red-tiled roofs of ordered rows of cottages. Here and there cows grazed. Then as the earth drew closer, a burst of small-arms fire abruptly disturbed the illusion.

Two of Major Wilson's men were hit before they touched ground, one of them killed; but the burst of opposition was as short-lived as it was out of place in the ordered Dutch setting. Wilson himself recovered from the impact with the earth to find himself looking up into the face of a German soldier, the German's hands already raised high in surrender.

As the main flight of troop carriers and gliders bearing British troops approached, brilliant-hued nylon panels marked their drop and landing zones. In one of the planes, a battalion commander, Lieutenant-Colonel John D Frost, spotted the panels soon after the red warning light came on.

Glancing about at his men, Frost noted 'the furious last-minute puffing at their cigarettes'. Then the green light went on, and the first of the men plummeted from the door, adding to a rapidly-growing panoply of parachutes dotting the sky. Moments later Frost himself was out. 'Once again the thrill of falling. The great relief of feeling the harness pulling and that highly satisfactory bounce as the canopy filled with air.'

From his glider, the division commander, General Urquhart – relieved that he had made the flight without air sickness – liked the look of the glider landing zone: flat, spacious, and screened by patches of pine woods. The countryside was much as he had imagined it from studying maps and aerial photographs. Off to the right, the shimmering broad ribbon that was the Neder Rijn. Up ahead, the city of Arnhem and the big road and rail bridges over the river. Closer, the tall smoke stack of an isolated factory near a surburban railroad station. Not far from it smoke billowing from a bombed building. Then Urquhart's attention shifted in grim fascination to the sight of the tow cord falling away from the nose of the glider, like something in a slow-motion movie, and the general braced against the pending impact of landing.

The air over the landing zone soon was thick with big Horsa gliders, their umbilical cords to their mother ships severed. While some glided smoothly toward the earth, others circled for landings. Some slid to relatively gentle rest in the big field. Others struck soft ground, sometimes coming to such an abrupt halt that the fragile craft flipped over onto their backs. Still others, their pilots having miscalculated distance or the amount of wind, overshot the field. In great rending, tearing crashes, wings clipped, they collided with pine trees in the woods or birches along the roads. In a few minutes the previously peaceful Dutch field presented a picture of frenzied disarray, as if some big-bodied plague had fallen from the sky.

Yet for all the disarray, an impressive 419 out of 454 gliders carrying British troops made it to the landing zone west of Arnhem, and casualties even in the most spectacular of the crashes were relatively few. The story was much the same with the Americans near Nijmegen and north of Eindhoven, where because of differences in tactical doctrine, the Americans depended for the initial landings less on gliders than on parachutes. In minutes, 16,500 Allied parachutists and 4,500 glidermen came to earth along a corridor in the Netherlands fifty miles long.

'What is it?' little Willem Haart, breathless from a race home on his bicycle, asked his grandfather.

'I don't know,' said the old man, 'but it looks like the end of the war.'

Armstrong Whitworth Whitley – the first of the RAF's 'heavy' bombers to go into service – did much valuable work at the beginning of the war. With the arrival of larger, faster and better armed aircraft, however, it was relegated to second line duties such as parachute training. Specification for Whitley Mk V: *Engines:* two Rolls Royce Merlin Xs, 1,075hp. *Armament:* five .303-inch machine guns and up to 3,500 pounds of bombs. *Maximum speed:* 230mph at 16,400 feet. Climb rate: 16 minutes to 15,000 feet. *Maximum* range: 2,400 miles. *Ceiling:* 26,000 feet. *Weights empty/loaded:* 19,350·/33,500 pounds. *Span:* 84 feet. *Length:* 70 feet 6 inches

Britain's first four-engined heavy bomber, the Short Stirling was beginning to reach obsolescence towards the end of the war, and the design was adapted as a transport and supply aircraft, also capable of towing gliders. Illustrated is a Mark III. The main difference between the earlier marks and the support aircraft, the Marks IV and V, was the deletion of armament entirely on the Mark V and all except the dorsal turret on the Mark IV. Specification is for Mark III. *Engines:* Four Bristol Hercules XVI radials, 1,650 hp each. *Maximum speed:* 270 mph at 14,500 feet. *Ceiling:* 17,000 feet. *Loaded weight:* 70,000 lbs. *Span:* 99 feet 1 inch. *Length:* 87 feet 3 inches

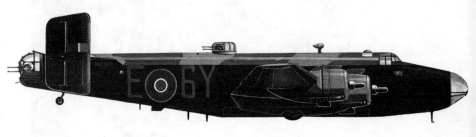

The Handley Page Halifax, like the Stirling, was widely used as a paratroop and glider aircraft as well as a bomber. Illustrated is a Halifax B III. *Engines:* Four Bristol Hercules XVI radials, 1,650 hp each. *Maximum speed:* about 300 mph. *Ceiling:* about 24,000 feet. *Loaded weight:* 65,000 lbs. *Span:* 104 feet 2 inches. *Length:* 71 feet 7 inches

The Airspeed Horsa was the main troop-carrying glider developed by the British and was used in the Sicily, D-Day and Arnhem landings. The fuselage could be swung into two parts to facilitate unloading. *Span:* 88 feet. *Length:* 67 feet. *Crew:* Two. *Load:* twenty-nine troops or a 75mm pack howitzer

The outcome of Operation Market

What Willem Haart and his grandfather saw was the start of Operation Market, history's largest airborne operation. Before it was over, more than 36,000 American, British, and Polish troops were to land by parachute or glider. In another operation destined to be staged six months later, more troops would arrive by air on the first day, but more airborne troops overall participated in Market.

The plan was the product of Field-Marshal Sir Bernard L Montgomery, charismatic commander of the 21st Army Group, which embraced the First Canadian and Second British Armies. Montgomery devised it as a means of cutting off Germans in the western part of the Netherlands, outflanking the border fortifications of the Westwall, and putting the Second Army across the major water obstacles in the Netherlands and in a position to drive deep into Germany along the North German Plain.

More than that, Montgomery looked on the plan as a way to convince the Supreme Allied Commander, Dwight D Eisenhower, to adopt his proposal for extending the great pursuit and bringing the war swiftly to an end. Put all the Allied resources, Montgomery insisted, behind the Second British and First US Armies in 'one full-blooded thrust' northeastward into Germany in the direction of Berlin. That, he argued vehemently, would prompt a tottering German command to capitulate.

Using three divisions of a recently created First Allied Airborne Army, Montgomery proposed to spread a carpet of airborne troops along a narrow corridor fifty miles deep while a fourth division – a British 'airlanding' division – arrived later in transport planes at the airfield north of Arnhem. The bridges over the big water obstacles secured, the Second Army was to pass swiftly through the corridor and proceed beyond Arnhem to the Ijssel Meer (Zuider Zee), a total distance of ninety-nine miles. The code name for

Lieutenant-General Sir Miles Dempsey,
Second Army commander

Field-Marshal Sir Bernard Montgomery,
21st Army Group commander

the ground attack was Operation
Garden.

Unmoved by the argument for a
single thrust into Germany, General
Eisenhower nevertheless listened
sympathetically to the concept of
Market-Garden. The Allied logistical
apparatus was too stretched, Eisenhower believed, to support any immediate end-the-war offensive, but
he still hoped to get a bridgehead over
the Rhine before supply shortages
forced his armies to pause. Market-Garden offered that promise.

Furthermore, ever since the break-out from Normandy, Eisenhower had
sought an opportunity to use the
idle airborne troops, only to see each
project cancelled by the rapid strides
of the ground columns. He was aware,
too, that the US Army's Chief of
Staff and the head of the Army Air
Forces were anxious to see the airborne troops tested in a strategic
role. The elite forces were, in effect,
coins burning holes in the Allied
command's pocket, and though Eisenhower had no intention of spending
them rashly, he was alert to any
sound opportunity to buy.

He gave his blessing to the operation.

Montgomery's plan was probably
the most daring, unorthodox plan
the Allies executed during the war.
It depended upon slender resources –
three lightly-armed airborne divisions, an airlanding division, and
one armored and two infantry divisions, the latter constituting the
only part of the Second Army that
had yet drawn up to the Dutch-Belgian frontier. How slender the
resources were was typified by the
remark of a senior British officer:
'We may be going one bridge too far.'

A basic premise behind the plan
was that the long and hasty retreat
from France had left the Germans
thoroughly disorganized, that even
though there were indications that
reinforcements were arriving to take
position behind canal and river lines,
the incoming troops were few and
ill-trained. Yet there were disturbing
last-minute reports. Reconnoitering
aircraft pilots noted heavy rail activity at Nijmegen and Arnhem, and
the Dutch Resistance reported battered panzer formations arriving in
the Netherlands to refit. So disturbed by the reports was the Second
Army commander, Lieutenant-General Sir Miles Dempsey, that he went
to Montgomery to push the view that
it would be better to drive northeastward close alongside the American First Army than to go off on a
tangent northward into the Netherlands.

Dempsey might have spared himself the trouble. Two days before, the
first flurry of the enemy's big supersonic rockets – the devastating V-2
– had fallen on London. The Germans
were launching them from bases near
The Hague. The War Office, Montgomery told Dempsey, had just sent

Major-General Roy E Urquhart, 1st Airborne Division commander

Major-General BC Freyberg, in command for the defense of Crete

him a signal asking what could be done to capture or cut off the bases. That made a drive northward into the Netherlands imperative.

The fact that the reports of increasing German strength actually were true further narrowed the chances of Allied success. The reinforcements digging in behind the canals and rivers were either the vanguard of the First Parachute Army or first arrivals of the Fifteenth Army. The latter had been pinned against the Channel coast when the Canadians had captured Antwerp, but the bulk of the troops escaped by ferrying in small craft across the Schelde estuary to the Dutch mainland. The rail activity and the word of arriving panzer formations signified the presence of Willi Bittrich's II SS Panzer Corps with the 9th and 10th SS Panzer Divisions.

A fanciful story, which later gained some credence, had it that the Germans moved the panzer divisions in response to word of Allied plans provided by a Dutch traitor, a big man adept with the girls known as 'King Kong' (after a gorilla in a motion picture of the same name). It made a good spy story, but Field-Marshal Model actually had ordered the divisions to the Netherlands on 3rd September, seven days before Montgomery and Eisenhower even decided on an airborne attack. Although the Dutchman brought word on the 16th to a minor German official that the British

were to resume their ground attack the next day and use airborne troops in support, the Germans discounted the information.

Operation Market took the Germans fully by surprise.

For all the surprise and success of the airborne landings, troubles quickly began to develop. Since the British drop and landing zones were six to eight miles from the primary objective – a great highway span over the Neder Rijn at Arnhem – getting to the objective on foot was a slow process. Hardly had the men begun their march when Dutch civilians turned out *en masse*, wearing orange, the national color, embracing the troops, pressing on them apples, tomatoes, flowers, and in their exuberance barring the route. It was carnival and holiday wrapped into one.

Dashing from the Hotel Tafelberg (spilling a hastily-packed suitcase in the process), Field-Marshal Model rushed by staff car to General Bittrich's headquarters, there to find that Bittrich already had acted to commit the two SS panzer divisions. He sent one to block the British from getting to the big bridge over the Neder Rijn in Arnhem, while the other hurried across the bridge and moved southward. Although Bittrich at the time had no knowledge of the American landings, he knew that if British ground troops were to establish contact with the paratroopers at Arnhem, that was the direction from

which they would have to come. So confident were the Germans of eventual success that they made no plans to destroy the highway bridges at either Arnhem or Nijmegen, though they did demolish the railroad bridge at Arnhem.

Despite Bittrich's moves, as night came Colonel Frost and just under 500 men finally gained the north end of the bridge over the Neder Rijn; but the Germans held firmly to the south end. Try as they might, no other British troops were able to push through to reinforce Frost's little band. While Major Krafft's youths and old men from Waldfriede harried the British rear, troops of the 9th SS Panzer Division holed up in the buildings of Arnhem and formed a hasty but effective screen against further British advance. At the north end of the bridge, Frost and his men were soon under siege by armored cars and tanks.

At Nijmegen the difficulty soon to face the Americans of the 82nd Airborne Division was less immediately apparent. In large measure because of the chance landing of Lieutenant Thompson and his six men almost astride the south end of the bridge over the Maas river near Grave, that vital objective was soon in hand. So was a crossing over the Maas-Waal canal between the Maas and the Waal. The paratroopers also moved swiftly to seize high ground southeast of Nijmegen, one of the few elevations to be found in the polderland of the Netherlands. The division commander, General Gavin, deemed the high ground vital if his men were to hold until the British ground column got through to them. So critical did he judge the high ground that not until nightfall did he spare a battalion from the job of securing it to move on another objective that would be critical if the ground column was to get past Nijmegen and reach Arnhem: an imposing highway bridge over the Waal river at Nijmegen.

In the first hours after the landings, only a few sentries had stood in the way of American capture of the Nijmegen bridge. As an American force finally moved toward the bridge,

first contingents of the 10th SS Panzer Division rolled across it and quickly fanned out in defensive positions inside the city. The bridge was destined for long, painful, costly hours to remain out of Allied reach.

Men of the 101st Airborne Division meanwhile had been securing almost all bridges over canals and smaller rivers between Grave and Eindhoven along the lone northward-leading highway that British ground troops would have to use; but they failed at one, a canal bridge closest to Eindhoven, which German defenders blew in their faces. The paratroopers nevertheless secured the approaches to the bridge and the next day would march almost unopposed into Eindhoven to the cheers of a populace that had festooned the city with the national color.

Unknown to the Americans, another event had occurred that was to speed German reaction to the airborne assault materially. As Gener-

Left: Paratroops mark a dropping area with a parachute.
Below: Reinforcements pour in

Left: British patrol in Oosterbeek. *Above:* A week after the airborne assault, British forward units were still isolated. *Below:* The column moves up

3-inch mortar squad in action

al Student from the balcony of his commandeered cottage watched the streams of aircraft and gliders passing overhead – his surprise tinged with envy at the vast resources available to the Allied command – anti-aircraft fire struck one of the gliders, and the craft plummeted into a field not far from the cottage. Rushing to the glider, German troops found the occupants dead. From the pocket of one, a German soldier pulled a sheaf of papers. It was a copy of the Allied operational order. Within two hours after the first parachutists had dropped, the order was on Student's desk.

Another misfortune befell the Allied operation when British ground troops ran into trouble trying to break through the crust of resistance that had formed in front of them south of Eindhoven. According to the plan, the ground column was to reach Eindhoven before nightfall on the first day, but when darkness came, the British armor was stalled six miles away. If the ground column was to reach the British airborne troops at Arnhem within four days – which was as long as those who planned the operation believed the parachutists and glidermen could hold out – a drastic reversal of fortune would have to occur.

The dawn of a new day brought little encouragement, for it ushered in a siege of inclement weather that delayed and in some cases precluded airborne resupply and reinforcement. From that time on, despite valor and sacrifice in such volume that the story might be told to the sound of trumpets, nothing the airborne troops could accomplish would be enough to alter the pattern of failure.

Nightfall was approaching on the second day, 18th September, before the British ground column finally fought a way into Eindhoven. It was after daylight on the third morning before the destroyed bridge over the canal north of Eindhoven was replaced. When in mid-morning the ground troops at last reached Nijmegen, they found German defenders

Top: American reinforcements land on fields littered with gliders from the initial assault. *Right:* German surrender, a rare British success at Arnhem

still holding the highway bridge over the sprawling Waal river.

Only late in the fourth day – Wednesday, 20th September – after a hastily-mounted assault crossing of the Waal's 1,200-foot width by American paratroopers using flimsy little canvas assault craft, did the Germans relinquish the big span at Nijmegen. Even then diehard defenders clung like beggar lice to the superstructure and underpinnings. The fifth day was drawing to a close before even a small contingent of the British ground column was able to cross the river and renew the attack in hope of traversing a remaining ten miles and rescuing the British paratroopers at Arnhem.

The paratroopers – who wore jaunty maroon berets and called themselves 'Red Devils' – were by that time under a state of siege. Of Colonel Frost's original 500 men at the north end of the bridge over the Neder Rijn, only about fifty survived to try to escape individually or in small groups; and few of them succeeded. The Germans meanwhile had driven the rest of the 1st Airborne Division into a cruelly confined little horseshoe-shaped position hinged on a ferry site along the Neder Rijn and on the Hotel Tafelberg, whence Field-Marshal Model had fled so precipitously the first day.

Even as the Americans at Nijmegen on the fifth day – Thursday, the 21st – cleared the last Germans from the bridge over the Waal, the British tried to reinforce the 'Red Devils' by dropping a Polish parachute brigade south of the Neder Rijn. The Poles were to cross into the horseshoe by way of a ferry; but by the time the parachutists landed, German shells had sunk the ferry boat. Furthermore, the Germans had just driven the British from a hillock topped by a country restaurant on the west side of the horseshoe; from the hillock German guns commanded both the horseshoe and the river.

The only hope of reinforcing the 'Red Devils' lay at that point with assault boats accompanying the Brit-

Left: Supply container. *Right:* Despite some spectacular crashes on landing, most glider troops survived unharmed

ish ground column advancing from Nijmegen. That hope was faint, for even should the ground troops break through swiftly, how to cross the river in the teeth of German fire? So dismal appeared all chances that the Second Army commander, General Dempsey, cancelled all proposals for reinforcing the airborne troops with the airlanding division that was to have been flown in to the airfield north of Arnhem.

The task of the ground column was the more difficult because the ground between the Waal and Neder Rijn rivers is polderland, too wet and spongy to support the weight of tanks or even armored cars. To thwart the British attack, the Germans had but to block the main highway leading to Arnhem and a few secondary roads. The British were further handicapped by heavy German artillery fire on convoys plying the lone highway leading north from Eindhoven – 'Hell's Highway', the men of the 101st Airborne had christened it – which delayed reinforce-

ments and supplies. On the sixth day German ground attacks temporarily cut the highway.

Only on the seventh day – Saturday, 23rd September – did the British in any strength gain the Neder Rijn across from the embattled 'Red Devils'. That night and the next they tried to cross the river, but treacherous mud along the south bank and intense German shelling kept the reinforcement to a trickle.

Finally forced to acknowledge defeat, British commanders on the 25th authorized the paratroopers to withdraw. Hungry, thirsty, red-eyed, the surviving able-bodied among the 'Red Devils' wrapped their muddy boots in rags to muffle the sound of their footsteps and began after nightfall to run a gauntlet of German patrols to the water's edge. Over 300 wounded had to be left in the perimeter to the mercy of the enemy, while ten times that number already were in Dutch or German hospitals.

The night was mercifully dark, and a heavy rain fell. Quiet at first, the

Germans soon after midnight awoke to what was happening and began to shell the river banks. Patient despite the German fire, nervousness, fatigue, the cold rain, the men queued for an empty boat. As dawn approached, many braved a treacherous current to swim across; but at daylight, some 300 remained on the north bank.

Of approximately 9,000 who had fought north of the Neder Rijn, only 2,400 made their way out. Over 1,200 were dead, hundreds more captured. During the same period the two US airborne divisions together had lost 3,500 men in killed and wounded. Counting glider pilots and British ground troops, Operation Market-Garden cost the Allies 11,850 casualties.

The operation accomplished some of what Field-Marshal Montgomery had intended it to accomplish. It had gained an Allied corridor sixty-five miles deep into the Netherlands, including bridgeheads over the Maas and Waal rivers; but by the merciless logic of war, the operation was a failure. It had failed to gain a bridgehead over the last river, the Neder Rijn, or to split the Netherlands, or to outflank the Westwall, or to position the British for driving deep onto the North German Plain. Nor had it extended the great pursuit in a manner that might have impelled a supposedly tottering German command to collapse.

Much of the failure could be laid to dismal luck: the location of the SS panzer divisions, the presence of Model, Student, and Bittrich on the scene, the finding of the Allied operational order, the degenerating weather. Although the Allies had recognized that the weather is erratic in northwestern Europe in September, they had insufficient resources to have put all the airborne troops on the ground the first day; that was a tremendous disadvantage, for once

The Germans fight back

the first troops had arrived, the ace
of airborne attack – surprise – had
been played.

There were other problems as well.
Throughout the fight at Arnhem, the
British were handicapped by small
and inadequate radio sets, which
they had opted to use in order to make
more space in planes and gliders for
the soldiers themselves. Bowing to
concern about a heavy concentration
of German anti-aircraft guns close
to the highway bridge at Arnhem,
General Urquhart had selected drop
and landing zones so far from that
critical objective that even a modicum
of resistance might have thwarted
its capture.

All those factors contributed to
the failure. Yet despite them, the
operation still might have succeeded
had the British ground column attacked with greater élan south of
Eindhoven and north of the Waal
and had the commander of the 82nd
Airborne Division employed the risk,
verve, and vigor expected of airborne
troops and allotted at least a battalion for a *coup de main* against the
Waal bridge at Nijmegen. That the
commander had acted in accord with
prior plan approved by his superiors
in no way erased the fact or the
serious effect of the failure.

Whether a successful Market-
Garden would have achieved the long-
range effect Montgomery hoped for
would forever remain conjecture; but
probably not. Even though the Germans had no additional reserves to
move immediately against the British, and even though the airborne
landings whipped the German Führer,
Adolf Hitler, into a lather of concern
(what, Hitler railed, if the Allies
should drop airborne divisions to
seize him and his staff!), the Germans had displayed no evidence of
panic, no inclination toward rout or
mass desertion. Barring a complete
collapse, impoverished Allied armies
whose logistical tethers were strained
to the point of breaking, were in-
capable at the moment of accom-
plishing much more than they had
already achieved.

The Douglas C-46 Commando was originally intended as a civil airliner, but the project finally became almost wholly military. The C-46 served in large numbers with US forces, mainly in the supply role. *Engines:* Two Pratt and Whitney Double Wasp radials, 2,000 hp each. *Maximum speed:* 264 mph. *Range:* 1,600 miles. *Ceiling:* 25,000 feet. *Weight empty/loaded:* 27,664/45,000 lbs. *Span:* 108 feet. *Length:* 76 feet 4 inches

The Douglas C-47 Skytrain was derived from the famous DC-3 airliner of the 1930s. Its specially strengthened floor enabled it to carry large loads, and as a paratroop carrier it could accommodate up to twenty-eight fully-equipped men. *Engines:* Two Pratt and Whitney Twin Wasp radials, 1,050 hp each. *Maximum speed:* 230 mph at 8,500 feet. *Range:* 2,125 miles. *Ceiling:* 23,200 feet. *Weight empty/loaded:* 16,865/30,000 lbs. *Span:* 95 feet. *Length:* 64 feet 6 inches

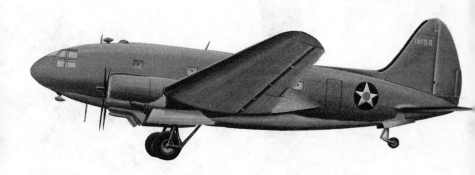

The WACO Hadrian glider was one of the mainstays of the US airborne forces. Capable of being towed at up to 125 mph, it was capable of carrying up to thirteen fully equipped men. *Span:* 83.3 feet. *Length:* 48.8 feet

Above: The Panzers mount their siege. *Below:* Some of the hundreds who were captured. *Right:* British casualty and comrade

The 75mm M20 lightweight collapsible recoilless rifle could be brought rapidly into action by paratroopers. *Weight:* 114.15lbs. *Length:* 6 feet 10 inches. *Maximum range:* 7,000 yards. *Muzzle velocity:* 1,000 feet per second. *Shell weight:* 13.19lbs. Complete round weight: 20.48lbs

Because of its light weight and toughness under all conditions in which it was used, the 105mm howitzer was a great favorite among the weapons of US artillery. *Rate of fire:* Four rounds per minute. *Range:* 12,500 yards

The 57mm M18 recoilless rifle folded down to little more than a simple tube for transport. *Length:* 5 feet 1⅝ inches. *Range:* 4,340 yards. *Muzzle velocity:* 1,200 feet per second. *Shell weight:* 2.75lbs. *Complete round weight:* 5.30lbs

The American 75mm pack howitzer was designed to be carried in gliders or in aircraft, and formed the main part of US airborne divisions' primary artillery support. *Weight:* 1,340 pounds. *Rate of fire:* Six rounds per minute. *Range:* 9,475 yards

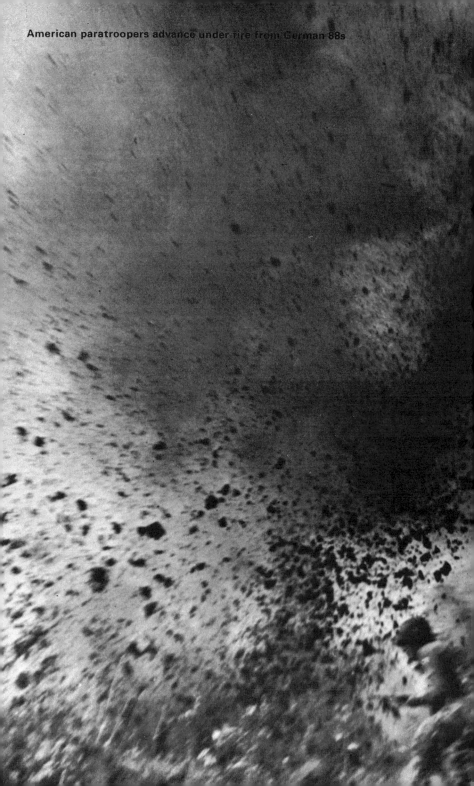

American paratroopers advance under fire from German 88s

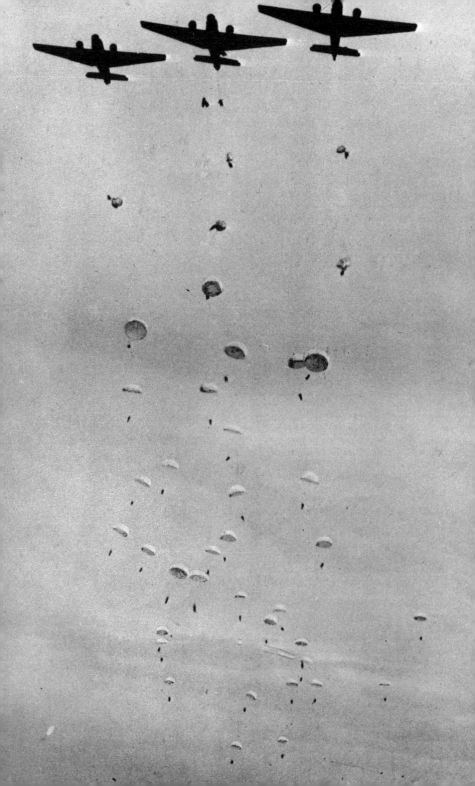

The rise and fall of the airborne forces

As history's largest airborne operation, the Allied descent from the skies on the Netherlands was the culmination of a prognostication that dated at least as far back as 1784, when Benjamin Franklin had written: 'Where is the Prince who can afford so to cover his country with troops for its defense, as that ten thousand men descending from the clouds might not, in many places, do an infinite deal of mischief before a force could be brought together to repel them?'

During the First World War Winston Churchill elaborated on Franklin's thesis, suggesting the dropping of 'flying columns' to destroy bridges, disrupt the enemy's communications, sabotage factories. During that same war an American, Colonel William ('Billy') Mitchell, who as a general officer later was to undergo courts martial for arguing the cause of airpower with too much vehemence, devised the first tactical scheme for an airborne attack. He intended giving a quick course in use of the parachute to men of the 1st Infantry Division, then drop them from British Handley-Page bombers behind the lines to take the city of Metz. The coming of the armistice forced cancellation of the plan.

As military dictatorships emerged in Europe and Asia and brought with them the threat of the Second World War, the means of airborne warfare were all on hand in fairly sophisticated form. The parachute, which dated from at least as far back as the 16th Century, had long been proven, and as early as 1927 the Italians had demonstrated a military applicability by dropping nine men at once with their equipment. All that remained to be done for the parachute was to change from silk to nylon. The sport of gliding having caught on in a number of countries, advanced models of gliders were available; and the planes developed by civilian airlines were adaptable to use as transports and troop car-

The DFS 230 troop carrying glider was developed by the main German
establishment dealing with the building and use of gliders. It was capable of being
towed by a Ju 52/3 aircraft at up to 100 mph and so that it could land in as short a
space as possible, it possessed three braking rockets in the nose and a parachute in
the tail. *Load:* Up to ten fully equipped troops. *Sink rate after release:*
240 feet per minute

riers. Throughout the Second World War, the Germans would employ an adaptation of a civilian model, the Junkers-52, and both Americans and British would depend primarily on the US civilian lines' DC-3 in a military adaptation called the C-47 Skytrain, or, as the British knew it, Dakota. Only in the later stages of the war was a plane specially built for airborne operations and then only in small numbers.

By the early 1930s, almost all the major armies of the world were experimenting to one degree or another with the idea of airborne operations, the Russians in particular. In 1934 the Russians staged a jump of forty-six men and dropped with them a small tank. Two years later, during maneuvers near Kiev, they astonished military attachés from around the world with a drop of two battalions. 'Locust warriors', the Russians called them. On 10th September 1936, at Minsk, 1,200 paratroopers jumped, and two weeks later, near Moscow, 5,200. The Russians also early perfected a military glider

capable of carrying eighteen men.

Yet paradoxically, as war came, the Russians were destined to make relatively minor use of airborne troops. They employed small bands of paratroopers on occasion during the Russo-Finnish War of 1939–40, but when the main contest began against the Germans, their elite airborne formations had to be committed as regular infantry in the crucial battle to halt the first German onrush on Moscow. Possibly because of the desperation with which the Red Army had to fight for a long time to come, these elite formations were never fully reconstituted. One reason was an acute shortage of transport aircraft that Russian factories were unable to provide if tanks and other priority items were to be produced in sufficient numbers.

The Russians made their most widespread use of the parachute in supplying bands of partisans that operated behind German lines and in dropping organizers to lead the bands. On a number of occasions they also dropped groups up to the size of battalions to destroy bridges or supply depots and to raid enemy airfields. Their basic task done, the men usually melted into the countryside to merge with the partisans.

In early October 1940, over a period of two days, transport aircraft shuttled approximately 6,000 troops to Russian-held airfields in the vicinity of Tula, just over a hundred miles south of Moscow, to thwart a German drive on that city, but that was an 'airlanding' as opposed to an 'airborne' operation. The Red Army staged only two major airborne operations during the war: the first near Vyazma, southeast of Moscow; the second near Kiev.

The operation near Vyazma was part of a counter offensive which the Red Army launched in December 1941, to throw back the Germans from the gates of Moscow. Over a period extending from 3rd January 1942, through mid-March, some 3,500 paratroopers and another 7,000 airlanded

Equipment drill for (left) Soviet and (below) German paratroopers

troops joined partisans and cavalry in an effort to cut German supply routes leading into a pocket formed by Russian counter offensives converging from north and south. The role of the paratroopers was to seize airfields for airlanding other troops, destroy bridges, and harrass German traffic on two main supply roads. Although the Germans had to shift major forces from other sectors and to fight for two months, they eventually destroyed the Russian force.

To tie down German troops and facilitate Russian crossings of the Dnieper river elsewhere, the Red Army, on 24th September 1943, began moving three airborne and three airlanding brigades to reinforce partisans in a great loop of the Dnieper southeast of Kiev. Misfortune plagued the operation from the start. Only 180 transport aircraft and a smattering of light gliders were available for moving the troops, and loss of aircraft to German fire and slowness in refueling sharply delayed the shuttling that was necessary. The first large batch of paratroopers to land

descended squarely on top of a German armored column, which cut the formation to pieces. Another force came down astride an infantry division and the corps headquarters the division was protecting; the Germans dealt harshly with that force as well. In the end, as at Vyazma, the Germans had to shift strength from other sectors to eliminate an airborne and airlanded force totalling 10,000 men. Thus, however chaotic the Russian operation, it achieved the goal of weakening the Germans elsewhere and did facilitate crossings of the Dnieper.

When news of the Russian airborne maneuvers of 1935 and 1936 reached Britain and the United States, it created considerable ferment among military theorists, but with few lasting results. Interest in both countries focused more on the air transport or airlanding concept – moving troops swiftly by air to already secure landing fields. As early as 1931 the Americans had flown men and guns of a battery of field artillery from one end of the Panama Canal Zone to the other, and the next year a British infantry battalion with full equipment flew from Egypt to Iraq. Yet as war approached, neither British nor Americans had any formal airborne establishment or even plans for one.

In Italy, too, despite the early experiment in 1927, the primary focus was on airlanding. In both the conquest of Ethiopia and the Spanish Civil War, the Italians on several occasions dropped supplies by parachute, and soon after entering the Second World War, they transported an infantry regiment in civilian airliners from Rome to an airfield in Albania. The first and only Italian airborne operation was launched on 27th April 1941, when a small band of parachutists seized the lightly defended Greek island of Cephalonia in the Ionian Sea.

Although the French in 1939 organized a battalion of paratroopers, they soon disbanded it. Only after the defeat of France in 1940 and the formation of the 'Fighting French' outside the country under the banner

Soviet troops exit from a hatch in the top of the aircraft

The Junkers Ju-52/3m was the maid of all work in the Luftwaffe, being used as a trainer, bomber, transport, liaison, paratroop and glider tug aircraft. A sturdy and reliable aircraft, the Ju-52 did invaluable work for Germany. *Engines:* Three BMW 132 radials, 830 hp each. *Maximum speed:* 189 mph. *Range:* 930 miles at 8,300 feet. *Ceiling:* 18,000 feet. *Weight empty/loaded:* 14,325/24,320 lbs. *Span:* 95 feet 10 inches. *Length:* 62 feet

The Gotha 242 was built in limited numbers as a troop carrying and cargo glider for the Luftwaffe, and eventually some models were built with engines. It had a crew of two and could carry a load of twenty-three men. Empty and loaded weights were 7,040 and 15,620 pounds respectively, while span and length were 72 feet and 52 feet

German paratrooper, a vital element in the successful 1940 campaigns

of Charles de Gaulle were the French to possess airborne troops. Portions of two battalions successfully parachuted into the Brittany peninsula as other Allied forces were coming ashore on D-Day in Normandy. The mission was to execute sabotage and then work with French resistance forces.

Before war came, the Poles and the Czechoslovaks also experimented briefly with airborne forces, and in the wake of defeat, Poland, too, was to have an airborne unit: a parachute brigade formed in England from Poles in exile, the 1st Parachute Brigade that saw brief action in Operation Market. The Japanese also experimented early, but for all the scale of their war effort, the Japanese once war came made small use of airborne troops. Not until the last month of 1941, as they started the war in the Pacific with the attack on Pearl Harbor, did they activate airborne units: the Yokosuka Special Naval Landing Force – a reinforced battalion of paratroopers – and the 1st Parachute Brigade, the latter composed of a reinforced battalion of paratroopers and an 'air regiment' of heavy bomber aircraft. They also formed another air regiment and an air transport corps.

The Japanese opened their offensive against the Dutch East Indies early in 1942 with a strike by sea and air on 11th January against Menado at the northwestern tip of Celebes. Four hours after a seaborne attack, the Yokosuka Special Naval Landing Force dropped by parachute on an airfield south of the city, took the Dutch defenders by surprise, and quickly secured the field. Just over a month later, on 14th February, the 1st Parachute Brigade jumped at Palenbang, on Sumatra, to capture two large oil refineries. Although the paratroopers quickly secured a nearby airfield, a mixed force of Dutch, Australian, and British troops held the refineries for two days until a Japanese seaborne force arrived to reinforce the paratroopers. A week later the Yokosuka Naval Landing Force staged another airborne operation in support of a seaborne assault to take the port of Koepang on the island of Timor. Neither assault encountered appreciable resistance.

That marked the virtual end of Japanese airborne operations. The Japanese had started too late to create the special forces required and to build large numbers of transport aircraft. Once the war was underway, other priorities prevailed.

Two minor operations on Leyte in the Philippines climaxed the Japanese airborne effort: in one, three Japanese planes crash-landed on 29th November 1944, in an attempt to raid rear echelon units of an American division, but those soldiers not killed in the crashes were quickly rounded up. In the other, on 6th December 1944, 300 Japanese parachuted in an effort to take over two US airfields. They destroyed some aircraft and briefly held one of the fields, but a planned seaborne reinforcement never arrived and American troops regained the airfield the same day.

It remained for the Germans to seize heartily upon the new airborne concept and to be the first to demonstrate its wartime potential forcefully and dramatically. In 1935, as Adolf Hitler denounced the military clauses of the Versailles Treaty, the head of the Luftwaffe, Hermann Göring, directed formation of the first German parachute units. Aside from the Russian demonstrations that year and the next, the Germans already knew of the Russian experiments by means of a separate military agreement within the framework of the Treaty of Rapallo of 1922. After hastily training a group of parachutists at a school near Spandau, the Germans sent fifty to fight with the Condor Legion in the Spanish Civil War, of whom twenty-three survived to bring back valuable observations. The Germans also acquired considerable airlanding experience during the same war in transporting Moroccan troops and their equipment in their tri-motored Junkers-52 planes.

As the Luftwaffe formed and trained parachute regiments and eventually (starting in 1939) divisions, only men with superb physical and mental qualifications were accepted. Like the men of the Waffen-SS, the military arm of the Nazi Party, the paratroopers were deeply indoctrinated in the tenets of National Socialism. A Luftwaffe general, Kurt Student – he who was later to envy Allied airborne resources – early took charge of the training.

The training under Student was physically and mentally strenuous. Aside from intense physical conditioning, the men underwent the usual infantry training, including extensive field maneuvers, and received special instruction in demolitions. At the school of parachuting at Spandau they made six jumps, the last under simulated combat conditions from aircraft flying below 400 feet.

Student formed his troops into conventional regiments of three battalions, each with three rifle companies and heavy weapons company. A platoon of thirty-six men flew in a flight of three aircraft. Combat dress included loose trousers, which bulged over the tops of high boots, a weatherproof gabardine coverall, and a thickly-padded helmet. The troops were armed either with an automatic rifle or a ; sub-machine gun (which American troops, from a high cyclic rate of fire that gave the weapon a guttural, emetic sound, were to call the 'burp gun').

In what now can be viewed as the preliminaries to the Second World War, the Germans launched their first airborne operation on 12th March 1938, when in the *Anschluss* against Austria airborne troops seized an airfield outside Vienna. Paratroopers landed first, followed by transport planes with men and heavy equipment, including field artillery. Eight months later Junkers transports airlanded an infantry regiment in a wheat field as part of the German occupation of the Czechoslovakian Sudetenland.

The Germans moved more slowly in adapting gliders to military use, despite the fact that during the years when Hitler paid lip service to the Versailles Treaty, civilian glider clubs with governmental encouragement proliferated. Thousands of young men who had learned the rudiments of flying in gliders later became Luftwaffe pilots. As war came in 1939, the Germans had a few military gliders, but not until 1941 did they form their

The long wait, inside a German transport on the way to Crete

first glider assault regiment. The basic German glider was the DFS-230, a high-winged monoplane with a length of just over thirty-seven feet, capable of carrying ten men. The Gotha-242 served as a back-up.

When the Germans started the war in September 1939 with the invasion of Poland, one false report after another of the use of parachutists emerged. In reality, although the Germans had an airborne force ready for use, so swift was the conquest that airborne troops were not committed.

The first combat use of German airborne troops was in the campaigns against Denmark and Norway opening on 9th April 1940. A company of parachutists early seized a vital bridge in what proved to be an uncontested conquest of Denmark. In Norway, in the first stroke of the campaign, airborne and airlanded troops seized airfields at Oslo and Stavanger. At Oslo, wave after wave of transport planes, machine guns pointing from their windows. landed without prior assault by parachutists, whereupon over 3,000 infantrymen moved swiftly to occupy the capital. At Stavanger a company of paratroopers landed astride an airfield, followed by 5,000 infantrymen landing in 250 transports. Far to the north, men of another company of para-

fields and erect fortifications around them. The full dramatic impact of the new form of warfare was to come only after a more striking demonstration in May 1940, when the Germans descended on the Low Countries and France.

While the Germans made their main effort through the Ardennes region of Belgium to break into northern France and strike swiftly for the Channel coast, the bulk of German airborne forces supported a secondary effort in the Netherlands. At The Hague, a battalion of paratroopers split to land on all three airfields ringing the capital and prepare for arrival of two-thirds of an airlanding division. The objective was the seat of government and headquarters of the Dutch High Command. In the meantime, four battalions of paratroopers and an airlanding regiment, all under the personal command of General Student, moved to take bridges over the Waal river at Dordrecht, the Maas at Moerdijk, and the Neder Rijn at Rotterdam for subsequent use by German ground columns.

At Dordrecht two platoons of parachutists quickly seized the bridge, then lost it to Dutch counterattack, to be regained only after ground troops, including tanks, arrived three days later. At Moerdijk the bulk of a battalion landed on both sides of the Maas river and quickly took two bridges intact, while at Rotterdam Student's main effort with two battalions of paratroopers seized an airfield outside the city for later airlandings. At the same time, a platoon of parachutists landed inside the city. As the men moved against the north end of the highway and railroad bridges over the broad Neder Rijn, an infantry company in six seaplanes landed on the river and taxied to the bridge abutments. After removing demolitions, the infantrymen joined the paratroopers to hold the north end of the bridge until ground troops arrived.

The Germans at The Hague had no such success, despite quick seizure of all three airfields. They lost the field north of the city to Dutch counterattack even after a battalion of reinforcements had landed in transports. The Dutch retook the

troopers landing outside Narvik were scattered badly in a poor drop, many of them injured. There Allied forces, including British troops, held out for two months before abandoning a last foothold. Meanwhile, a few days after the first landings, a company of paratroopers dropped ahead of advancing ground units to seize a railway station in central Norway. After another poor drop, only thirty-four out of 150 survived a siege by Norwegian forces that ended only after German ground troops arrived five days later.

These relatively small airborne assaults provoked no flurry of airborne activity in other countries, although in a number of cases commanders shifted troops to defend air-

other two fields before German reinforcements arrived, and although some transports landed on a nearby beach and a highway, Student was forced to divert subsequent flights to Rotterdam. The Dutch won at The Hague, though it would do them scant good in the long run in view of German success elsewhere and impending Dutch surrender in the field.

In the southern Dutch 'panhandle' around Maastricht and in Belgium, where the Maas is known as the Meuse, the Germans coincidentally launched a smaller but nonetheless spectacular airborne assault to seize bridges at Maastricht and over the Albert Canal farther south, plus a reputedly impregnable Belgian fortress on the Albert, Fort Eben Emael. Descending silently before daylight on 10th May in DFS-230 gliders, small German detachments seized two bridges over the Albert, lost another to demolitions, and took a damaged but still serviceable bridge over the Maas at Maastricht. Those bridges enabled a ground column to get in behind the Albert and the Meuse to the relief of other German troops that had landed full atop Fort Eben Emael. The men from the gliders were hard at work destroying the fort's turrets and casemates when after daylight 300 paratroopers jumped as reinforcements. Around noon the next day the Belgian garrison of over a thousand men surrendered.

With France and the Low Countries defeated and the British withdrawn bloody from Dunkirk, Hitler made provision in his tentative plans for invading Britain for Student's 7th Parachute Division to lead the way, although Student himself was temporarily incapacitated from a head wound incurred in the fighting in the Netherlands. Partly because of the Luftwaffe's failure to drive the Royal Air Force from the skies, partly because the German Navy could promise no decisive intervention by the Royal Navy, and partly because Hitler's mind was turning toward another foe to the east, the plan was never executed.

As it turned out, the next assignments for German airborne troops

German DFS 230 assault glider

were in Greece. If Hitler was to have a secure right flank for the swift campaign he intended against the Soviet Union, he had to go into Greece to the rescue of his headstrong ally, Benito Mussolini.

On 8th April 1941, a company of German paratroopers landed near Salonika in an attempt to disrupt communications behind the Metaxas Line, but most of the men were killed or captured. Not quite three weeks later, on 27th April as British, New Zealand, and Australian troops made a fighting withdrawal into the Peloponnesus as a first step in evacuating Greece following the Greek army's surrender, the airborne troops struck again. Two battalions of paratroopers – 1,500 men – reinforced by a glider-borne engineer company descended on the only bridge leading into the Peloponnesus, that over the Corinth Canal at Corinth. Although the British succeeded in blowing the bridge at the height of the battle, the effect of trapping a British brigade still on the mainland was much the same as if the Germans had captured the bridge intact. Fortunately for

the British, the Germans, in the belief that only a small rear guard still opposed them, failed to exert enough pressure to prevent the Royal Navy from removing most of the brigade through a small port on the mainland, while the Commonwealth and other British forces made their escape from the Peloponnesus.

The British evacuation of Greece prepared the scene for history's first large-scale airborne assault, one destined to have profound impact on the attitudes of the two sides – Allied and German – in regard to the future

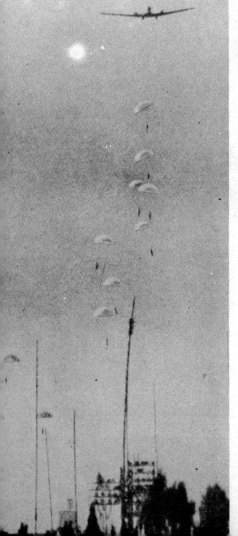

of airborne warfare. That was the German conquest of Crete, at once the zenith and the nadir of the German airborne.

Largest island in the Aegean Sea, Crete was a strategic prize for both sides. From its harbor near the western end of the island at Suda Bay – largest in the Mediterranean – the Royal Navy might conduct far-ranging operations. From its three airfields – arrayed along the north coast at Maleme on the west, adjacent to Suda Bay, at Retimo a few miles to the east, and at Heraklion, still farther east – the Royal Air Force could threaten southern Italy and the Balkans as far as the oilfields of Rumania while at the same time serving the British cause in Egypt and Libya. In German hands, the island would provide bases for the Luftwaffe to imperil British sea lines of communication through the Mediterranean and serve the German cause in Egypt and Libya, perhaps even provide a stepping stone for a strike by air and sea against the vital Suez Canal.

When the withdrawal from Greece occurred, the British, for all the importance of Crete, had accomplished precious little toward erecting defenses on the island. That was partly because until Mussolini invaded Greece in late 1940, Crete like the motherland was neutral. It was also because Britain's limited resources in the eastern Mediterranean were severely strained.

When Major-General Bernard C Freyberg stopped off – he thought temporarily – at Crete following his evacuation along with two-thirds of his New Zealand division from Greece, he learned that he had a new assignment: defend Crete. Aware of the presence of the enemy's 7th Parachute Division in Greece, the British high command was convinced that the Germans soon would hit the island with a combined airborne-amphibious invasion.

For the defense Freyberg had respectable numbers – 30,000 British and Commonwealth troops, 11,000 Greeks and Cretans – but the numbers were deceptive. They represented a hodge-

The Netherlands – Germany invades

The Netherlands

podge, most of them bits and pieces evacuated from Greece with only the guns and equipment the men could carry on their backs. Morale had suffered in the withdrawal while awe of apparent German power had grown. The two brigades of Freyberg's own New Zealand division were the strongest of the lot. Nor did the vital part of the island – the north coast with its airfields and harbor – afford good natural defensive barriers, though behind the northern littoral stood a range of rugged mountains across which little more than cart tracks led to the south coast.

By cannibalizing damaged guns, Freyberg managed to assemble forty-nine serviceable artillery pieces, and he had a few tanks, most of which were obsolescent light tanks that had already lived out their life expectancy in Libya. Because aircraft were so few as to represent no more than prey for German planes, Freyberg ordered them flown out. They departed on 19th May which – as it turned out – left no time for cratering or otherwise obstructing the runways against their use by German planes. Even had there been time, Freyberg had no authority to damage the fields: the British were so hopeful of holding Crete and building up strength there that Freyberg's superiors refused permission. There was one bright spot nevertheless: so obvious were the initial objectives – the airfields and the harbor – that Freyberg was able to concentrate such forces as were at his disposal in their defense.

From a suite in a luxury hotel in Athens, General Student personally planned and directed the invasion, which he himself had talked the Fuhrer into launching in order to demonstrate the value and prowess of his airborne force. Student had something over 500 Junkers transport planes, seventy-five gliders, and some 600 bombers, dive-bombers, and fighters. He had at his disposal 22,750 men, including the elite 7th Parachute Division. Some 10,000 men were to arrive by parachute (that would require three waves, with the transports returning each time to Greece

for a new load), 750 by glider, 5,000 in airlanding transports, and 7,000 in small craft by sea.

Since the airfield at Maleme was the largest of the three fields and the one closest to Suda Bay, Student allotted the first wave to it, an assault force of paratroopers and glider infantry totalling upwards of 2,500 men. One battalion had the specific objective of taking a low height, Hill 107, which dominated the Maleme airfield. Once the airfield was secure, most of the troops to be airlanded were to arrive there.

Components of a size roughly equal

Crete – 'the grave of the German paratroopers'

to that at Maleme were to take the airfields at Retimo and Heraklion, though they were to arrive only in the second and third lifts. Having had experience thus far only in small-scale airborne operations, General Student planned, in effect, three separate relatively small-scale assaults, for which he could count on surprise only for the first one. At the same time he held out no parachute reserve. If the first and primary assault at Maleme should fail, Student would be in trouble: he had to have the Maleme airfield to bring in the transports, and the Royal Navy in the Aegean was powerful enough to give any seaborne assault a difficult time.

Despite a heavy pre-assault bombardment by German bombers and Stuka dive-bombers, the main assault on 20th May at Maleme gave every indication at first of failure. Although the gliders in the vanguard for the most part made successful landings, the parachutists came down full astride the defense positions of Freyberg's New Zealanders. To the paratroopers floating downward, the earth that rushed up to meet them was alive with deadly tracers from

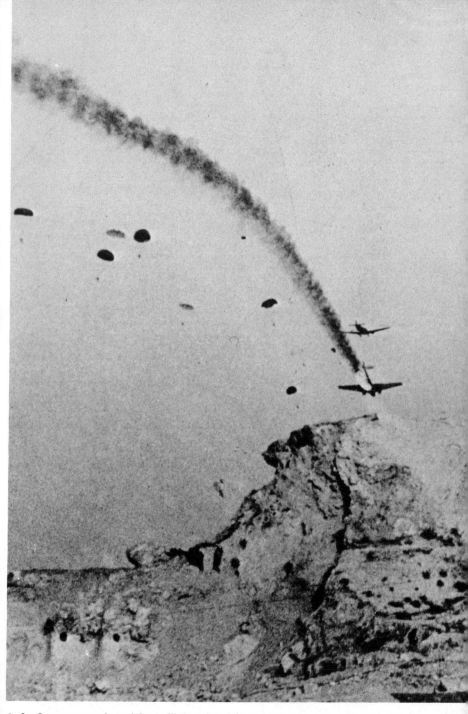

Left: Germans equipped for a flight with flotation jackets. *Above:* A transport comes to grief over Crete

Above: The glider troops who went to Mussolini's aid on Gran Sasso.
Right: Mussolini with his rescuers

rifles, Bren guns, Lewis guns, 40mm Bofors anti-aircraft pieces. Dangling helplessly in their harness while awaiting impact with the ground, the paratroopers fought back as best they could with their sub-machine guns. The war was suddenly no mammoth confrontation of massed armies but a deadly game of individual against individual.

Two-thirds of one German battalion was wiped out. In the face of that development, the German regimental commander deemed he had to commit almost everything left him to take Hill 107, for without that dominating height, holding the airfield itself would avail him nothing.

The commander of the 22nd New Zealand Battalion had two companies on Hill 107, the other two on the airfield below. In the furor of battle, he lost communications with the two on the field and assumed them overwhelmed. As pressure grew against his own position on the hill, he asked reinforcement, only to learn that none was available. When an attack to relieve his position failed, he began to despair. As night came, all his mortars and machine guns

were out of action. On a radio so rapidly weakening that it was good for but one more transmission, he told his brigade commander that he deemed it imperative to withdraw.

No matter how exigent the New Zealanders' situation – in point of fact, the 'missing' companies down on the airfield were fairly well off – that of the Germans was even more so. The regimental commander lay wounded, his force of 1,900 men reduced to a mere 600. Having come to earth atop another New Zealand position six miles away, another band of paratroopers had incurred such losses that the commander had decided to dig in rather than move on the airfield. The planes returning to Greece for the follow-up waves were sharply reduced in numbers – some shot down, others failed mechanically – so that only portions of the forces scheduled for the airfields at Retimo and Heraklion could be moved. Even those were long delayed by the necessity to service and refuel

the planes. As the darkness deepened, neither the airfield at Retimo nor the one at Heraklion could the Germans claim.

When during the night the paratroopers on the lower slopes of Hill 107 roused themselves for a new assault, they were sure they would encounter the same cruel fire they had experienced throughout the day. With each cautious step they waited for it to begin, but it failed to materialize. Slowly, stealthily, warily, the Germans crawled forward. With incredulity they found the Allied positions empty, the entire hill theirs for the taking.

No one could have said so with any finality at the time, but with the evacuation of Hill 107, Crete was lost. An Allied counterattack during the night got no place. Starved for information and fearful of the worst, General Student sent a pilot at daylight to land a Junkers-52 on the airfield at Maleme regardless of the situation, then to radio Student the outcome. Although the plane took some hits, the pilot succeeded in landing, talked with paratroopers on

the field, then took off again. The Germans were free to send in reinforcements, the word was, because Hill 107 was in hand.

Student promptly ordered in every paratrooper left to him, which because of the loss of transports and the delays on the first day, made a considerable force of 600 men. Those were soon on their way to jump over the Maleme airfield while airlanding troops got ready to follow as soon as the transports returned.

As night fell on the second day – 21st May – officers and men of neither side could yet discern the outcome. The Germans, for their part, were depressed when after dark, outside Suda Bay, a great clamor arose, a thunder of big guns: British ships were destroying the first of two waves of German seaborne reinforcements. Such a thorough job did they do that the second wave turned back. That afforded new hope to General Freyberg and his men. A counterattack Freyberg ordered against the Maleme airfield the next morning might prove decisive.

The hope proved stillborn. In the

face of the German reinforcements, the counterattack ground to a halt short of the airfield, and all the while Junkers-52s continued to land, to disgorge troops, and take off again. Before it was over, 22,500 Germans had come to Crete, and as the third day neared an end, General Freyberg already had begun contemplating a fighting withdrawal across the mountains to the south side of the island.

In the end, Freyberg would accomplish that by means of desperate and violent combat against overwhelming odds. Yet when the Royal Navy extracted the last of 17,000 men it was able to bear to safety, thousands more remained trapped on Crete.

As the last of those who escaped pulled away on British vessels on the night of 30th May, and as those who remained accepted the ignominious but ineluctable fact of surrender, the sins of the defenders were fairly ob-

Left: Hitler inspects the glider troops who took the Belgian Fort Eben Emael. *Below*: Another inspection, this time by Göring

Another 'stick' jumps into Crete. One in four German paratroopers died

vious. Facing a new confrontation only weeks after the retreat from Greece, having few prepared defenses and little support (none from the air), and encountering a new, apparently overwhelming concept of warfare, Freyberg and his subordinates had fought the battle from the first under the cloud of a pervasive sense of impending defeat. They had dealt the enemy a crippling first blow, but they had failed the crucible of decisive counterattack.

To the vanquished, the enemy's mistakes and the Pyrrhic nature of his victory were less apparent, but they were nonetheless real. General Student had planned the campaign less as one mammoth airborne assault than as three small ones, all of roughly equal strength despite the overriding importance of the airfield at Maleme. Only because not all of his paratroopers made it to Crete on the first day (the schedule was overambitious in the first place) did he possess an airborne reserve to reinforce those who fought for the primary objective at Maleme. Even then he well might have failed had not the New Zealanders so ill-advisedly abandoned Hill 107.

Furthermore, the price of victory was oppressive. 4,000 Germans died,

airborne attacks on the Russian front, but for one reason or another – mainly the pace of the Red Army's advance – none came off. All the remaining German airborne operations were in the west and none was of appreciable size.

On the night of 14th July 1943, a battalion of German paratroopers jumped over southeastern Sicily to reinforce defenders of a critical bridge, but British paratroopers by chance dropped almost atop the Germans a short while later and took the bridge. On 11th September 1943, in the wake of Italian defection from the Axis, a battalion of German paratroopers jumped near Monte Rotondo and attacked an Italian headquarters. A general cease-fire between German and Italians soon ended the fighting.

The next day a small German glider force landed on a mountain in northern Italy and rescued the Italian dictator, Benito Mussolini, who was being detained by a government that had gone over to the Allied side. Shortly thereafter the German 2nd Parachute Division jumped onto the island of Elba and encountered only a modicum of opposition. Two months later, after British troops had occupied several of the Dodecanese Islands in the wake of Italian surrender, a battalion of German parachutists with the help of seaborne forces retook Leros Island. On 21st July 1944, 200 German glider troops landed in the Vercors region of southeastern France to counter an uprising by French resistance forces and with the help of ground troops suppressed the insurrection.

A final foray by German airborne troops remained. Delayed twenty-four hours by shortage of fuel for a war-weary fleet of Junkers-52s, less than a battalion of paratroopers dropped near Malmédy in the Belgian Ardennes on 17th December 1944, as part of Hitler's counteroffensive to wrest a new initiative on the Western Front – the 'Battle of the Bulge Badly scattered in the jump and hampered by a lack of roads and trails in a region of high marshes, the paratroopers never coalesced, and American troops swiftly hunted them down.

It was an ignoble end for a once-proud arm of the Wehrmacht.

including one out of every four of the elite paratroopers, and total losses exceeded thirty per cent. Concerned as early as the time of the invasion of France and the Low Countries that the vital element of surprise might have gone out of airborne assault, Hitler saw Crete as proof that the days of the paratroopers were over. Although he was to become less sure of that in the months to come, Crete prompted him to send most of the elite airborne troops to bleed to death in ground combat in Russia.

Crete, said Student, was 'the grave of the German paratroopers'.

In the remaining years of the war, the Germans planned several small

Crete

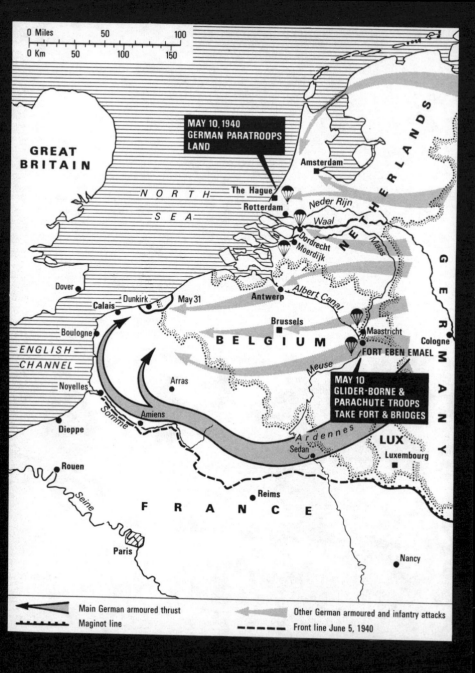

MAY 10, 1940
GERMAN PARATROOPS
LAND

GREAT
BRITAIN

NORTH

SEA

NETHERLANDS

Amsterdam

The Hague

Rotterdam

Neder Rijn

Waal

Dordrecht

Moerdijk

Maas

GERMANY

Dover

Dunkirk

May 31

Antwerp

Albert Canal

Calais

Brussels

Maastricht

Cologne

Boulogne

BELGIUM

FORT EBEN EMAEL

ENGLISH
CHANNEL

MAY 10
GLIDER-BORNE &
PARACHUTE TROOPS
TAKE FORT & BRIDGES

Noyelles

Arras

Meuse

Somme

Amiens

Ardennes

LUX

Dieppe

Sedan

Luxembourg

Rouen

Reims

FRANCE

Seine

Nancy

Paris

→ Main German armoured thrust

→ Other German armoured and infantry attacks

▪▪▪▪ Maginot line

- - - - Front line June 5, 1940

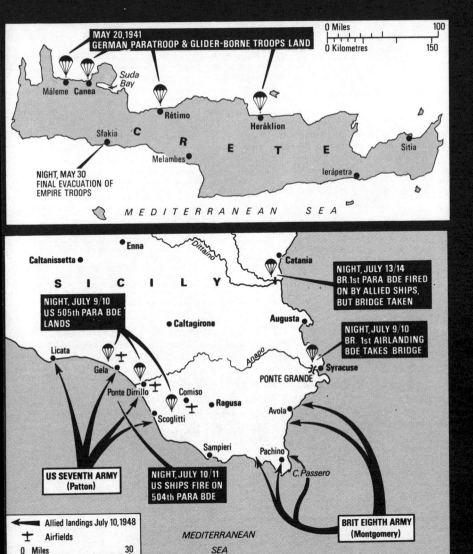

Top: Crete

MAY 20,1941
GERMAN PARATROOP & GLIDER-BORNE TROOPS LAND

0 Miles 100
0 Kilometres 150

Máleme Canea
Suda Bay
Rétimo
Heráklion
Sfakia C R E T E Sitia
Melambes
Ierápetra

NIGHT, MAY 30
FINAL EVACUATION OF
EMPIRE TROOPS

M E D I T E R R A N E A N   S E A

Below: Sicily

Enna
Ditaino
Caltanissetta
Catania
S I C I L Y
NIGHT, JULY 13/14
BR.1st PARA BDE FIRED
ON BY ALLIED SHIPS,
BUT BRIDGE TAKEN

NIGHT, JULY 9/10
US 505th PARA BDE
LANDS

Caltagirone
Augusta
Anapo
NIGHT, JULY 9/10
BR. 1st AIRLANDING
BDE TAKES BRIDGE

Licata
Gela
Syracuse
PONTE GRANDE
Ponte Dirrillo
Comiso
Ragusa
Avola
Scoglitti
US SEVENTH ARMY
(Patton)
Sampieri
Pachino
NIGHT, JULY 10/11
US SHIPS FIRE ON
504th PARA BDE
C.Passero

BRIT EIGHTH ARMY
(Montgomery)

Allied landings July 10, 1948
Airfields
0 Miles 30
0 Kilometres 40
MEDITERRANEAN
SEA

Left: The Germans Attack: 1940. *Top:* Crete. *Below:* Sicily

Early Allied developments

American and British military leaders read the outcome of the invasion of Crete in terms diametrically opposite from Hitler's. To the two powers that eventually were to form the coalition destined to crush Hitler in the west, the airborne assault on Crete was vindication of steps to create airborne forces that both had taken in the wake of the airborne successes in the Netherlands and at Fort Eben Emael. Crete further spurred their efforts.

On 22nd June 1940 – three days before France succumbed to the Nazi colossus – the Prime Minister of Great Britain, Winston Churchill, had contacted the head of the Military Wing of the War Cabinet Secretariat. 'We ought to have a corps of at least five thousand parachute troops ... ' Churchill wrote. 'I hear something is being done already to form such a corps but only, I believe, on a very small scale. Advantage must be taken of the summer to train these forces who can none the less play their part meanwhile as shock troops in home defence ... '

Churchill's brief followed by some two weeks a decision by the Air Ministry to establish a parachute training center at Ringway, the civil airport for Manchester in the industrial north . As a result of the brief, the War Office ordered to Ringway a major of the Royal Engineers, John F Rock, 'to take charge of the military organization of British airborne forces'.

Major Rock's assignment was at first as discouraging as his orders were vague and brief. It came at a time when invasion of Britain appeared imminent, when all British military and industrial facilities were severely strained, when any digression from the basic task of turning back the Luftwaffe's violent assault from the air seemed peripheral if not downright wasteful. Although the airborne forces were to be a part of the army, they would depend on the Royal Air Force for their parachute instructors and for their aerial transport. Those were things a Royal Air Force pre-

American paratrooper, a highly trained and efficient volunteer

occupied with the nation's survival was slow to provide.

The Central Landing School (later the Central Landing Establishment) had to make do at first with meager resources, including six venerable Whitley bombers, from which parachutists had to exit not from a side door, as was preferable, but from a hole in the floor created by removing half the rear gun turret. ('The Elephant', British paratroopers called the ponderous Whitley, which led to an obvious nickname for the aperture from which they jumped). Since the British aircraft industry was tied up with orders for fighters and bombers, the Whitleys or other bombers would have to suffice until American industry could provide the C-47 Dakota.

At this same time, the first of the British Commando units that were to conduct raids on the Nazi-held Continent were being formed. Since it seemed logical that one way to transport the Commandos to their assignments was by air, the first troops to undergo parachute training were from one of the new Commando battalions.

By 1st August, little more than a month after the impetus provided by Churchill's brief, every man of the Commando battalion had completed three qualifying jumps – the first one from a balloon that swayed giddily and discouraged all but the most hardy from going through with the maneuver. Renamed the 11th Special Air Service Battalion, the Commandos staged their first mass drop in November. Fifty men jumped from four Whitleys over Salisbury Plain. Among the distinguished observers was Crown Prince Olaf of Norway, whose limousine the paratroopers – unaware of the eminence of the owner – commandeered to speed them to their ground objective.

Less auspicious was the beginning of another demonstration staged in April of the following year before another battery of distinguished guests, including the Prime Minister. Over a loudspeaker set up to enable the visitors to hear the commands, the director of the demonstration asked: 'Hallo, formation leader, are you ready to take off? Over to you.' 'No,' came the answer. 'I'm not. Five of the chaps have fainted.'

Despite that humorous – if embarrassing – delay and despite high winds, the parachutists staged another successful demonstration that did credit to a growing airborne establishment. In charge now was Major-General F A M ('Boy') Browning as General Officer Commanding Airborne Troops. The original training center at Ringway was supplemented by another at Hardwick, and plans were underway for creating before the end of the year the 1st Airborne Division, of which the 11th Special Air Service Battalion, rechristened the 1st Parachute Battalion, was to be a part.

In keeping with the British system of maintaining permanent regiments to which a number of battalions can be added or withdrawn depending upon the need to expand or contract the nation's forces, all battalions of both the 1st Airborne Division and another division to be created later were a part of what became known as the Parachute Regiment. As members of that regiment, all British paratroopers were authorized to wear a distinctive headgear, the Red (actually maroon) Beret, and a shoulder patch depicting a heroic Bellerophon astride the winged horse Pegasus. Eventually reaching a strength of seventeen battalions, the Parachute Regiment constituted an elite force of volunteers meeting stringent physical and mental requirements. In consideration of the hazards of their assignment, the men received extra pay of two shillings a day.

Aside from the beret, distinctive shoulder patch, additional pockets, and a semi-waterproof outer smock, the men of the Parachute Regiment wore the standard British soldier's uniform. For taking extra equipment into battle, they often jumped with a kit bag strapped to one leg by a long cord. Individual weapons were much the same as those of line units but with an extra helping of automatic weapons: Bren light machine guns and Sten sub-machine guns.

Meanwhile, in late 1940, the Ministry for Aircraft Production had placed the first order for gliders – 400 Hotspurs, prototype of the Horsas and Hamilcars that were to follow; but not until well into 1942 were gliders to be available in appreciable numbers.

In final form the Horsa was a high-winged monoplane sixty-seven feet long with a wing span of eighty-eight feet and a tricycle undercarriage that could be jettisoned in favor of a central skid. It possessed a thin skin of plywood attached to circular ribs of stouter wood. Although the Horsa could transport cargo as bulky as jeeps and anti-tank guns, it was primarily a troop carrier with seats arranged along the length of both sides of the fuselage. The Hamilcar was basically a freight carrier capable of handling loads as heavy as a light tank. Freight could be loaded and unloaded through a hinged nose. Both types were towed at first by the Albemarle bomber and later by Stirling and Halifax bombers and the C-47.

As the British airborne division gradually evolved, it contained two parachute brigades of three battalions each, an 'airlanding' (glider) brigade that at first had only two battalions but subsequently received a third, an airlanding light regiment of Royal Artillery equipped with 75mm pack howitzers, and contingents of engineers, medics, and other services, including a light tank squadron. The parachute battalions had three rather than the usual four companies.

In the United States, development of an airborne force in many ways paralleled that in Britain.

Small-scale experiments with dropping parachutists and weapons at airfields in Texas in the late 1920s had had little lasting effect. Not until 1938 did serious theoretical discussion of airborne operations begin after the Command and General Staff College at Fort Leavenworth introduced the subject in its curriculum. The next year the Chief of Infantry proposed creating an airborne force, a proposal that precipitated a debate for control of the new arm.

The infantry saw airborne troops merely as infantrymen transported by air to battle. The Corps of Engineers based a claim on the theory that the men would serve primarily as demolition experts and saboteurs. Making a strong pitch, the Army Air Corps held that airborne troops should be 'air grenadiers' in the same way that Marines served as a ground adjunct of the US Navy.

Above Left: Major-General WC Lee. *Above right:* Major-General RN Gale
Right: Lieutenant-General FAM 'Boy' Browning, GOC British Airborne Troops, confers with Major-General James Gavin, commanding 82nd US Airborne Division

The matter was still undecided when in June 1940, three days after Churchill's brief directing creation of a British airborne force, the War Department ordered formation of a parachute test platoon. As in Britain, a major, William C Lee, an early exponent of the airborne concept, headed the new program. Two months later the Chief of Infantry won control.

The test platoon went first to Hightstown, New Jersey, to the locale of the Safe Parachute Company that had built the parachute tower in the amusement park at the 1939 New York World's Fair, there to practice on the company's experimental towers. When the tests proved successful, the platoon moved to The Infantry School at Fort Benning, Georgia, where modified replicas of the original parachute tower were erected.

As did the thrill seekers at the fair, the soldiers descended in a parachute that was already open and was controlled by rigid wires, but then they moved on to another tower from which they floated to earth beneath a parachute which, though already open, had no mechanical controls in the descent. Training jumps from B-18 bombers and later C-47s followed.

The parachute test platoon led in early fall of 1940 to the creation of a parachute battalion, the 501st, with a strength of 446 officers and men. Despite considerable enthusiasm for

the new force, the War Department was slow to create additional units, primarily because of a shortage of transport aircraft. Almost a year after the birth of the 501st Parachute Battalion, the United States had only sixty-six C-47s, only twelve of which could be spared for the paratroopers. Under the impetus of the German invasion of Crete, the War Department nevertheless activated three more parachute battalions before the year 1941 was out, along with two air-landing battalions.

A shortage of parachutes also slowed training, a factor complicated by War Department insistence that all US paratroopers be equipped with a second emergency parachute. As it turned out, the Americans were the only airborne force in the Second World War to carry the emergency device.

As in Britain, the American paratroopers were an elite force of volunteers, mentally and physically well above the average soldier. The airborne also early adopted badges of distinction, a metal insignia of a parachute with winged embellishments and high-topped 'jump boots' that set the men apart from regular infantry. The men also early adopted a distinctive song to the tune of the Battle Hymn of the Republic: 'Gory, gory, what a helluva way to die!'. They were a hardy lot, so spoiling for a fight that they often took on their infantry comrades while on leave in

Above: The objective at Brunéval
Right: Homeward bound after the raid

Columbus, outside Fort Benning, or in the iniquitous commercial dens across the Chattahoochee River in Phoenix City, Alabama.

Not all received extra hazardous duty pay at first. Officers and higher ranking non-commissioned officers qualified for the 'flight pay' earlier authorized for the Air Corps, but several months passed before Congress authorized 'jump pay' for all ranks – $50 a month for an enlisted man, $100 a month for an officer.

With the activation of additional parachute battalions, the War Department set up headquarters of a Provisional Parachute Group, again headed by Lee (promoted to lieutenant-colonel), and founded the Parachute School as a subsidiary of The Infantry School. As the War Department underwent a thorough reorganization in the spring of 1942, a newly-created Army Ground Forces embraced a special Airborne Command, again with Lee in charge. Lee's command supervised airborne training and coordinated with an equivalent Troop Carrier Command in a redesignated Army Air Forces.

The inhibitions on training imposed by the shortage of transport aircraft sharply restricted the number of airborne troops that could participate in maneuvers. Not until November 1941 were enough planes assembled to transport an entire battalion at once. Enthusiasm for the new concept nevertheless remained high, as reflected in a glider program instituted by the Army Air Forces following the invasion of Crete. When experiments in the summer of 1941 proved promising, the Air Forces with characteristic American dash and fervor in less than two years trained more than 10,000 glider pilots and contracted for more than 13,000 Waco CG4A gliders. Comparable in size to the C-47, the Waco could carry only fifteen men as compared to the thirty-two carried by the British Horsa.

Glider infantry at first received neither extra pay nor any distinctive uniform or insignia, which furthered a rabid jealousy between the infantry-

men and the paratroopers. At one post a poster appeared with photographs of wrecked gliders and the words: Join The Glider Troops! No Flight Pay – No Jump Pay – But Never A Dull Moment. Not until the spring of 1944, shortly before the invasion of Normandy, did Congress authorize flight pay for the glider infantry that matched the jump pay of the paratroopers.

Having considered at first that airborne troops would fight only in small units, usually on sabotage missions, the man who could be called the father of the American airborne, Bill Lee, had by the end of 1941 begun advocating airborne divisions. Although the proposal drew many supporters, the trained resources were yet too few. In February, 1942, the War Department nevertheless directed formation of four parachute regiments. Each regiment was to receive as its first component one of the four existing parachute battalions, whose numerical designation passed to the regiment. The 501st Parachute Battalion, for example, became the 1st Battalion, 501st Parachute Infantry.

The man who had to be sold on the airborne division was the Chief of Army Ground Forces, Lieutenant-General Lesley J McNair, a crusty though stalwart personality who advocated a minimum of specialized units so that in a global war, divisions with only a few modifications might operate effectively anywhere they were called upon to serve. McNair at first looked upon the airborne division not as a true division but as a task force to be assembled when needed by combining parachute regiments with standard forces trained for the occasion in air transport, much as the Germans had supplemented the 7th Parachute Division for the invasion of Crete.

When in the spring of 1942 the War Department began contemplating an invasion of Europe the following spring and included an airborne division in the planning, McNair contemplated using an infantry division that would undergo special airborne training. Only after Bill Lee – advanced now to the rank of brigadier-general – went to England and brought back news of British plans for airborne divisions, did McNair reconsider. While approving creation of two airborne divisions, he insisted that they have a minimum of overhead and transportation and constitute, in effect, an infantry division in miniature. With the decision, out went the concept of separate units specially trained in the techniques of airlanding; those already formed were converted to glider infantry.

As conceived and approved in late summer of 1942, the airborne division totalled only 8,500 men, as opposed to some 15,000 in the infantry division. Two divisions were activated – the 82nd and 101st – each with one parachute infantry regiment and two glider infantry regiments, a ratio about which McNair and Lee differed sharply, but McNair's view prevailed. The economies in numbers were achieved in part by sharp restrictions on the amount of ground transportation but also by reductions within the tactical units: the glider infantry regiment had only two battalions and two platoons per company; the parachute platoon had only two rifle squads and a machine gun squad; and there were only three parachute field artillery battalions.

Individual weapons were similar to those of regular infantrymen except for more automatic weapons, such as the Browning Automatic Rifle (BAR), the 'Tommy-gun' (Thompson submachine gun), and the 'grease gun' the latter so-called because it looked like a device for servicing automobiles. Division artillery consisted of thirty-six 75mm pack howitzers, although later one of the parachute battalions would be converted to a 105mm= glider battalion. Having no organic aircraft, the divisions depended for movement on transport planes of the Army Air Forces' Troop Carrier Command.

At dusk on 10th February 1941, eight Whitley bombers took off from Malta, two loaded with bombs with orders to create a diversion, the other six carrying thirty-eight men of the 11th Special Air Service Battalion. The objective was to cut an aqueduct in southern Italy that carried the main water supply of the province of Apulia, including that of such cities as Taranto, Brindisi, and Bari. The British were putting their new airborne force to a test in its infancy.

Five of the six Whitleys bearing paratroopers dropped their loads close to the appointed spot while the men in the sixth came to earth in the next valley, too far away to participate in the demolition. Supply bundles assembled, the main body of paratroopers fixed explosives to the aqueduct and took cover to await the blast. They hardly could have hoped for greater success. A great gush of water poured from the aqueduct to course down the valley of the little Tragino creek.

The next part of the operation was more difficult: to traverse some fifty miles of mountainous terrain and gain the west coast near the town of Salerno, where four nights later His Majesty's Submarine *Triumph* was to be lying off the mouth of the Sele river to spirit the raiders away. Breaking into three parties, the men moved by night and took cover by day, but for all their precautions, none of them reached the coast. The countryside had been alerted to their presence, and Italian troops and *carabinieri* were too diligent in their search.

Perhaps it was just as well that all were captured, for had they reached the mouth of the Sele, they would have encountered cruel disappointment. By incredible coincidence, one of the Whitleys that had participated in the bombing to create a diversion had made a forced landing near the mouth of the Sele. Unaware of the plans for the submarine, the pilot radioed his plight. Because the British command assumed the Italians had intercepted the signal and would send troops to the Sele, the orders to the submarine were cancelled.

Meanwhile, in the Near East, the British had formed another Special Air Service Battalion. On the night of 17th November 1941 – the eve of a British offensive in the Western Desert – fifty-four men of that battalion set out in five obsolete Bombay aircraft to execute sabotage against Axis airfields. A wind that came up after the troops were airborne grew so strong that none of the men came to earth any closer than ten miles from an objective. Only twenty-one of the fifty-four men subsequently made their way to a planned rendezvous with a long range desert patrol and thence to safety. Although Greek and Iraqi troops trained by this battalion executed several other small-scale airborne raids in later months along the coasts of the Eastern Mediterranean, the battalion itself restricted its remaining operations to the ground.

Three months after the desert raid, on 27th February 1942, the British staged their third parachute assault, again in the tradition of the Commandos. The commander was a man who was to distinguish himself in many another airborne assault as the war went on – John D Frost, at the time a major. The objective was an underground concrete shelter near the village of Bruneval, one of several along the French Channel coast containing a radio-detection apparatus that British intelligence was anxious to learn more about. Major Frost and 118 others were to parachute almost atop the German installation, photograph some parts of the radar device, dismantle others for scientists in England to study, then take German beach defenses in rear and rendezvous with landing craft that were to transport them to gunboats lying off shore.

Two of three contingents of Frost's force landed right on the target, while the third came to earth close enough to enable the men to join the others after only a brief delay. Paratroopers were astride the radar shelter before the Germans awoke to what was happening. In a sharp exchange of small-arms fire, two of the British parachutists were killed; but a few hours later all the others, except for six men who got lost in the darkness, were clambering aboard landing craft on the nearby beach, vital parts of the enemy's radar set in tow.

As the British executed their third airborne assault, most American airborne troops had become a part of either the 82nd or 101st Airborne Divisions and were entering their first weeks of divisional training. An exception was the 2nd Battalion, 503rd Parachute Infantry (later to be redesignated the 509th Parachute Infantry Battalion). In April 1942, that battalion arrived in England to complete its training alongside the British airborne units.

When Allied planners in early fall of 1942 began creating the design for invading French North Africa – with the goals of bringing the French protectorates back into the war, eventually linking with British forces in Libya, and making the Mediterranean safer for Allied shipping – they included no provision at first for airborne troops in the assault. The target date of 8th November was only a month away when the vital necessity for gaining aerial superiority in case the French should remain loyal to their puppet government in Vichy and oppose the invasion, focused attention on two airfields in western Algeria near Oran.

The assignment of seizing the airfields fell to the 2nd Battalion, 503rd Parachute Infantry, under Lieutenant-Colonel Edson D Raff. Raff's men were to fly 1,500 miles from England to North Africa. Ironically, in what was destined to be the longest uninterrupted flight by airborne troops during the war, the crews of the C-47s were woefully inexperienced. Most pilots were civilian airline pilots hastily mustered into uniform; some had received their planes only a few hours before the flight; many had never flown in night formation; and some of the navigators had joined the crews only a few days before. Furthermore, after flying such a distance, the planes would have to land close behind the paratroopers or else run out of fuel.

Just what kind of a reception the paratroopers might expect at the two French airfields – La Senia and Tafaroui – was in doubt. As the men took off in thirty-nine C-47s after nightfall on 7th November, they had no inkling whether they would land to the accompaniment of French cheers or drop by parachute on a landing zone between the two fields and march against French guns. They were supposed to learn the answer by a radio signal as they flew across the Strait of Gibraltar, but that signal was never heard.

In the face of fog and the difficulties of night flying, the planes early began to lose formation, but with the coming of dawn thirty-two of the thirty-nine were at least still within sight of each other. Of the others, one landed at

Gibraltar because of engine trouble, two landed far from the target in French Morocco, three landed in Spanish Morocco, and a seventh dropped its paratroopers over Spanish Morocco. All together, sixty-one para-troopers were interned by the Spanish authorities.

The occupants of the main group of planes got their first indication of the reception awaiting them when they arrived over La Senia airfield as Allied planes were bombing it. In the confusion that followed, the men in twelve planes jumped between the two airfields, while most of the others landed with their planes on a dry lake bed several miles from La Senia. Before any of the airborne troops reached either of the two airfields, a motorized American ground force that had arrived over beaches near Oran occupied both.

It was an inauspicious opening combat assault for American airborne

Combat memento, complete with bullet hole

troops, but in a matter of a few days they were destined to do better. As Allied forces began a race to the east in hope of seizing Tunisia before Axis troops could enter in force, a battalion of British paratroopers under Lieut-enant-Colonel R J Pine-Coffin – the vanguard of the 1st Parachute Brigade – made an unopposed drop on 12th November to help take the small port of Bône, while three days later Colonel Raff and the 400 of his men he was able to assemble after the first abortive action jumped to seize a French air-field a hundred miles inland at Youks-les-Bains. Armistice negotiations having been concluded, the French at the airfield welcomed the paratroopers enthusiastically.

The next day another battalion of the British 1st Parachute Brigade met a similar reception after jumping at the crossroads settlement of Souk-el-Arba inside Tunisia on the main road to Bizerte. Then, in a last desperate effort to win the race for Tunisia, a third battalion of the brigade under John Frost (promoted to lieutenant-

colonel) jumped in advance of a British armored thrust near the Depienne airfield, south of Tunis. From this field, which intelligence had revealed had been abandoned, Frost moved overland fifteen miles to seize the airfield at Oudna, only ten miles from Tunis.

That field, too, Frost found, had been abandoned; but the next morning, as Frost's men entrenched to defend the periphery, German dive-bombers roared in, machine guns spitting, while on the ground infantry counterattacked with the support of tanks. Meanwhile, the attack by British ground troops had faltered, coming to a halt a full fifty miles from the embattled paratroopers at Oudna.

Colonel Frost had little alternative but to fight it out through the day, then in darkness to sneak away and hope to cross fifty miles of rugged mountainous terrain to safety. For four days and nights the paratroopers marched, seeking to elude the strafing of persistent German aircraft, engaging in one fierce ground clash after another with German forces, fending off hostile Arabs who, like vultures, trailed the column in eager resolve to strip those left behind – dead and wounded alike – of equipment and clothing. In the end, Frost and 180 men made it out, but 266 others were lost.

Except for a raid on 26th December by thirty men of Colonel Raff's battalion aimed at demolishing a railroad bridge behind German lines in eastern Tunisia (only six men, including two French guides, made their way back), that ended the airborne operations in North Africa. That is not to say that for either Raff's battalion or the 1st Parachute Brigade was the fighting ended. Both American and British airborne troops stayed on for long weeks, plugging gaps in a thin Allied line, fighting alongside regular infantry units, absorbing heavy losses. Before the last of the airborne troops were pulled from the line in April 1943, the British brigade alone had lost 1,700 men – killed, wounded, and missing. Only a steady stream of replacements had kept their ranks anywhere near full strength.

In the meantime, thousands of miles away, the British had launched another small-scale but potentially important airborne operation. On 19th November 1942, transport planes released two gliders over Norway carrying troops to attack a German heavy water plant, which British intelligence had deduced had to do with experiments in atomic energy. One of the gliders crashed into a mountain, while the other crash-landed. All survivors were captured and later poisoned or shot on the order of Adolf Hitler.

By the time the Allies were ready to stage their next invasion – the island of Sicily in July 1944, in hopes of driving the Italians from the war or at least of gaining a stepping stone to the Italian mainland – Allied airborne forces had multiplied. The British were creating another division, the 6th, which included a battalion of Canadians. The Americans had activated their third division, the 11th, and a fourth, the 17th, was in prospect. The 101st was engaging in maneuvers in the United States, the 82nd was in North Africa, as was the British 1st, and a separate regiment, the 503rd Parachute Infantry, had been sent to the Pacific. For two of the divisions, the 82nd and 101st, the Americans had changed the organization: now they had one glider regiment to two parachute regiments, instead of the reverse. The change was based less on tactical concepts than on a shipping shortage that made it difficult to get gliders overseas. In both Britain and the United States, shortages of troop carrier aircraft and gliders continued to hamper airborne training.

In planning for the invasion of Sicily, Allied commanders counted on a reinforced 505th Parachute Infantry of the 82nd Airborne Division to jump in advance of the US Seventh Army's seaborne assault and seize high ground behind invasion beaches on Sicily's southwestern coast, thereby to shield the beaches from counterattack. The British 1st Airlanding Brigade was to arrive in gliders behind invasion beaches on the southeastern coast, capture a bridge called the Ponte Grande near the port of Syracuse, help in taking the port and silence a coastal battery.

This largest airborne assault yet

staged by Allied forces had much going against it from the start: American pilots of the 51st and 52nd Troop Carrier Wings, who were to fly in the American troops and tow most of the British gliders, were gravely inexperienced in night flying, and the route the planners designated in an effort to stay clear of the anti-aircraft guns of naval convoys carrying the seaborne force was complex, involving three sharp changes of direction while the pilots were flying over the sea in darkness.

The British glider infantry was first to take off from airfields in Tunisia the evening of 9th July. Seven of the 144 gliders failed even to clear the North African coast, and once over the Mediterranean the other planes and gliders encountered gale-force winds that turned the usually placid sea into a gyrating thing topped with foam. Some squadrons were blown well to the east of the designated route, and others in the rear overran forward serials. Yet despite these troubles, ninety per cent of the aircraft reached the southeastern tip of Sicily, then swung northeast on a prescribed zig-zag course in search of the glider release point off the coast near Syracuse. Possibly as many as 115 planes carrying 1,200 men started on that last leg of the journey, but few found the proper release point. Only fifty-four gliders landed in Sicily, and only twelve were on or even near the correct landing zones. The others fell into the sea with a loss of 252 men.

Of those who survived the debacle, less than a hundred were able to start marching for the objective, the Ponte Grande. That little band nevertheless seized the bridge. Although Italian forces eventually overwhelmed the paratroops, they failed to destroy the bridge. When British seaborne troops arrived in the afternoon, the bridge was still intact and again passed into British hands. Another small force of airborne troops successfully eliminated the coastal battery that was also an objective.

The American paratroopers, in the meantime, were experiencing less casualties but just as much confusion. Losing direction in the gale and missing check points, the troop carrier planes approached Sicily from all points of the compass, some flying full over the naval convoys but surviving because naval gunners held their fire. Hopelessly lost, two pilots turned back to North Africa, while a third crashed into the sea.

Once the bulk of the planes passed the coastline, German and Italian anti-aircraft fire further scattered the formations, and haze, dust, and smoke from a preliminary naval bombardment obscured all landmarks. The problem at that point became less one of getting the paratroopers to the correct drop zones than of getting them to the ground at all instead of in the sea. The 4,400 paratroopers who jumped scattered like wind-blown confetti, landing all over southeastern Sicily. Only one battalion hit the ground relatively intact, and even that unit was twenty-five miles from the designated drop zone.

Coming to earth, the men found themselves in a strange land bearing no resemblance to the maps and aerial photographs they had studied. Their commander, slender young Jim Gavin, at the time a colonel, was not even sure at first that he was in Sicily.

Coalescing in small groups, the paratroopers had little choice but to follow the age-old maxim of marching to the sound of the cannon. In that way most moved gradually toward the Seventh Army's invasion beaches, cutting enemy telephone wires, engaging small groups of Germans and Italians wherever met, and creating confusion among enemy commanders as to where the main airborne landing had occurred. Yet only 200 men were on the assigned objective, the high ground behind the invasion beaches whose possession might mean success or failure in repelling enemy counterattack.

For all the lack of numbers, that little group succeeded in delaying attacking Italian infantry until a battalion of the seaborne force could reach the high ground. That battalion was then able to stop German infantry that struck the hill later and to call on naval gunfire to halt German tanks.

When the Germans on the second day by-passed the high ground, they came close to pushing some of the

American units into the sea until newly arrived American tanks and artillery brought the counterattack to a halt. Yet despite the temporary success, so shaky was the American beachhead that the commander, Lieutenant-General George S Patton, Jr, called for airborne reinforcements to arrive the second night, 11th June.

Although the word went to ships off the coast and to anti-aircraft units ashore that slow, low-flying C-47s would be arriving close to midnight, that did little to forestall the catastrophe that followed. After two days of crisis in the beachhead, the troops ashore were jumpy, and the sailors supporting them were wary of anything that flew, such punishment had they absorbed from German planes.

Into the uneasy calm following a German air raid on the Allied ships flew the planes carrying 2,000 paratroopers of the 504th Parachute Infantry. The first wave made it without incident, but as the second serials approached, somewhere a lone machine gun opened fire. That signal set off almost every anti-aircraft gun on and off the shore.

'Planes dropped out of formation and crashed into the sea,' a surviving paratrooper recalled. 'Others, like clumsy whales, wheeled and attempted to get beyond the flak, which rose in fountains of fire, lighting the stricken faces of men as they stared through the windows.'

Of 144 planes that had departed Tunisia, twenty-three never returned, and thirty-seven were badly damaged. A total of eighty-one men died; sixteen were missing and presumed dead; and 132 were wounded.

Two nights later troops of the British 1st Parachute Brigade winged toward Sicily in transports piloted by Americans to seize a bridge over a river and speed a British attack on the port of Catania. Again anti-aircraft gunners aboard Allied ships opened fire. They cut down two transports and forced nine others to turn back after pilots were wounded or planes badly damaged. The others were badly scattered, and when German anti-aircraft gunners also opened up, what little regimen remained in the formations dissipated. Ten more planes turned back, and thirty-seven

either went down in flames or crashed into the sea.

The pilots of the surviving planes had little choice but to drop their paratroopers or release their gliders whenever and wherever they could. Out of 1,900 men who went in, only some 200 reached the bridge, there to discover that they had dropped almost on top of a battalion of the enemy's 1st Parachute Division, which had come to earth only a few hours earlier. Incredibly, the little band of British airborne troops managed to seize the bridge and either hold it or keep it under controlling fire until British ground troops arrived.

Despite the confusion and tragedy that plagued Allied airborne operations in Sicily, at least one German commander, Kurt Student, believed the airborne contribution to the invasion was 'decisive'. 'If it had not been for the Allied airborne forces blocking the Hermann Göring Panzer Division from reaching the beachhead,' Student said after the war, 'that division would have driven the initial seaborne forces back into the sea.'

No non-partisan witness in any case where airborne troops were involved, Student clearly was engaging in hyperbole. The panzer division had posed no overall threat to the Allied beachheads, in no way affecting the British and causing genuine concern to only one of three American divisions. The Allied paratroopers had nevertheless made a valuable contribution to the invasion, probably more than they themselves recognized, for their scattered landings had thoroughly confused many an Axis commander. Their performance so impressed Adolf Hitler that he questioned whether he had been right in so summarily downgrading his airborne forces after Crete.

Yet Allied commanders expected more than that of the elite airborne troops. Indeed, the outcome of the airborne operations in Sicily prompted many an Allied leader – particularly among the Americans – to question the feasibility of large-scale airborne assaults.

On the American side of the Atlantic, Sicily even put the continued existence of airborne divisions in the United States Army in jeopardy.

The path to D-Day

Among those who questioned the viability of the airborne division after Sicily was the overall Allied commander in the Mediterranean, Dwight D Eisenhower.

'I do not believe in the airborne division,' General Eisenhower wrote to the US Army's Chief of Staff, George Marshall. Dropping an entire division, Eisenhower believed, would of necessity scatter the troops over such an extended area that the division commander might find it impossible to regain control. In any case, he went on, if airborne troops were organized in smaller, self-contained units, a senior commander with a small staff and communications facilities could always be dropped to insure necessary coordination.

Even more dubious was the Chief of the Army Ground Forces, Lesley McNair. General McNair saw the confusion and high losses of the Sicilian landings as proof of his earlier stand against forming what he called 'trick outfits'. McNair proposed that the airborne divisions be broken up, making the parachute regiments into non-divisional units and bringing the other contingents together as light divisions that could be given quick specialized airborne training should the need arise for an airborne force the size of a division.

The man in charge of British airborne troops, General Browning, disagreed: he saw the problem as basically one of coordination and control between the transport units and the airborne troops, which could be solved by creating an airborne army in command of both. Although a special board convened by the US War Department did not go that far, it nevertheless advocated a drastic overhaul of airborne training to enable troop carrier and airborne units to work together at considerable length before entering combat. 'The activation and training of airborne units are related directly to the activation and training of troop carrier units,' the board noted, which was a roundabout way of

Gliders drawn up with their distinctive
D-Day marking

urging the Army Air Forces to make greater effort to facilitate joint training. In reply, the Chief of the Air Forces, General Henry H Arnold, promised increased emphasis on equipping and training troop carrier units, especially in night operations.

The fate of the 'trick outfits' was still in abeyance when on 5th September 1943, the independent 503rd Parachute Infantry that had deployed to the Pacific staged an impressive daylight operation. In eighty-four C-47s and in company with an Australian

Demonstration drop by 1,500 troops, watched by Churchill and Eisenhower

parachute artillery battalion equipped with 25-pounder guns, the regiment took off from Port Moresby in New Guinea. To assist a three-pronged Australian drive for the Japanese-held port of Lae, the paratroopers were to seize an airstrip at Nadzab, some twenty miles inland, as a preliminary step in blocking Japanese retreat. An Australian division was to arrive in transports beginning the next day.

A lack of opposition made the operation hardly comparable to Sicily, yet the coordination between airmen and airborne troops was impressive nevertheless. A-20 Havoc medium bombers

laid smoke screens to hide the drop zones. Big B-25 Mitchell bombers bombarded the landing area, while B-17 Flying Fortresses, specially equipped for the purpose, dropped bundles of arms and equipment by parachute. Meanwhile, P-38 and P-47 fighter-bombers flew aerial cover.

The operation was 'completely successful'. Perhaps, after all, noted observers back in the United States, there was a future for large-scale airborne operations if only the proper coordination could be achieved between the parachutists and the crews of the planes. The Secretary of War, Henry L Stimson, called on leaders of the army to study the organizational set-up of the New Guinea operation.

Although improved joint training clearly was a prerequisite for solving the problems, there were steps to be taken also in improving navigational aids. The 82nd Airborne Division took such a step in the next American airborne operation, a hastily-mounted airborne reinforcement of a hard-pressed American beachhead on the Italian mainland on the shores of the Gulf of Salerno.

Crisis precipitated by German counterattack mounted in the beachhead the night of 11th September 1943. Commanding the US Fifth Army, Lieutenant-General Mark W Clark the next day called for help by whatever means. Since it would take several days to move reinforcements from Sicily by sea, General Eisenhower authorized the 82nd Airborne Division to drop paratroopers into the beachhead.

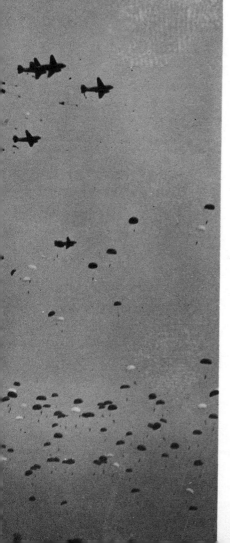

Three planes carrying special teams called 'pathfinders' preceded the main airborne force. Once on the ground, the pathfinders set up portable lightweight radar sets, while to circumvent any repetition of the tragic events over Sicily, orders went to every Allied anti-aircraft gunner on ship and shore that nobody was to fire under any circumstances against any plane, German or Allied.

Before daylight on the 13th, 1,300 paratroopers dropped with unaccustomed accuracy into the beachhead, almost atop a giant 'T' formed by flaming drums of oil. Ironically, their dramatic arrival had little effect on the crisis in the beachhead; for near midnight on the 12th, before the first paratroopers arrived, the ground troops themselves had at last halted the counterattack, and the Germans had begun to fall back.

That the Germans were thwarted was less readily apparent at the time. The night of the 13th additional airborne troops dropped into the beachhead, and the redesignated 509th Parachute Infantry Battalion got ready to drop near Avellino, twenty miles beyond the periphery of the beachhead to block roads over which the Germans presumably were moving reinforcements.

Hastily-mounted, the drop at Avel-

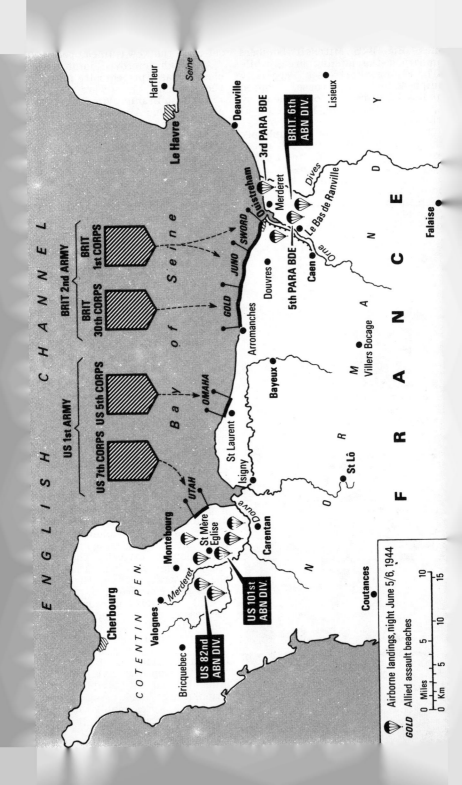

ENGLISH CHANNEL

Seine
Harfleur
Le Havre
Deauville
Lisieux

BRIT 2nd ARMY
BRIT 1st CORPS
BRIT 30th CORPS

Bay of Seine

3rd PARA BDE
BRIT. 6th ABN DIV.
Ouistreham
Merderet
Dives
Le Bas de Ranville
5th PARA BDE
Orne
Caen
Douvres
Falaise

SWORD
JUNO
GOLD

US 1st ARMY
US 5th CORPS
US 7th CORPS

OMAHA
Arromanches
Bayeux
Villers Bocage
St Laurent
Isigny
St Lô

UTAH
Carentan
Douve
St Mère Eglise
Montebourg
Merderet
US 101st ABN DIV.
US 82nd ABN DIV.
Cherbourg
Valognes
Bricquebec
COTENTIN PEN.
Coutances

FRANCE

Airborne landings, night June 5/6, 1944
Allied assault beaches

0 Miles   5   10
0 Km   5   10   15

GOLD

lino was ill-starred from the first. No pathfinders were employed because high mountains and the distance beyond the beachhead made the little radar sets that were available at the time useless. Because of the mountains, it was impossible to drop the men from a preferred height of 400 to 600 feet; and from altitudes of 1,000 feet and more, Avellino and the other hamlets in the area – the pilots found the night of 14th January – looked much the same. The planes sowed the paratroopers as broadly as they had in Sicily, here and there over a hundred square miles. The battalion commander himself came down in the middle of a German tank park and was quickly captured. Small groups nevertheless got together, blew bridges, cut communications wires, and ambushed small parties of Germans. All but just over a hundred of the 640 men who jumped filtered back eventually to Allied lines, but the overall effect of the operation was muted.

That the airborne units were available as a reserve for the Salerno beachhead was a result of cancellation of one of the most audacious airborne operations planned during the course of the war. It was designed to capitalize on the surrender of Italy by seizing the capital of Rome with Italian connivance and assistance and thereby hopefully forcing the Germans to evacuate the southern half of the Italian peninsula.

Sixty-two C-47s were already airborne with troops of the 82nd Airborne Division when Brigadier-General Maxwell D Taylor, the division's artillery commander who had gone secretly to Rome to arrange details of Italian cooperation, used a prearranged radio signal to cancel the operation. The operation was risky in any case, but Taylor had found the Italian high command vacillating and indecisive about the Italian role. Ten months were to pass before Rome came into Allied hands.

In the United States and in Britain, in the meantime, efforts continued to improve coordination between troop carrier and airborne units and otherwise to correct the deficiencies Sicily had pointed up. A special effort went toward providing all transport aircraft and airborne units with pathfinder and navigational radar and with VHF (Very High Frequency) radios, the latter to afford communication between the airborne troops and the troop carriers once the troops had landed.

Because of acute shortages of radar equipment in the United States, most of the new pathfinder techniques were worked out by British and Americans together in Europe. As eventually developed, the technique involved pathfinder teams of ten men dropping around thirty minutes before the first serials, just long enough to afford the men time to set up their equipment. The standard marking for drop zones was a T formed by five lights and a radar set – the British-developed 'Eureka' – installed at the head of the T A 'Rebecca' beacon carried in the aircraft transmitted on the Eureka's frequency, to which the Eureka automatically replied and provided the aircraft a fix on its location in relation to the Eureka. For marking a glider landing zone, a line of seven lights of alternating colors was to be placed through the main axis of the landing area and a Eureka installed off the down wind side of the light. In the event of daylight operations, colored smoke also might be used.

To facilitate control and training, American troop carrier wings in Britain were brigaded together under the 9th Troop Carrier Command, a component of the Ninth Air Force. When the Ninth Air Force received a new commander, Lieutenant-General Lewis H Brereton, the troop carriers were bound to receive increased attention, for it was Brereton as a junior officer who had been charged with tactical planning for Billy Mitchell's proposed airborne attack on Metz in the First World War. In November, James Gavin, promoted to brigadier-general, arrived in England with orders 'to deal directly with Troop Carrier Command and the airborne divisions in order to get results

Although plans were underway in the United States to create a fifth airborne division – the 13th – doubts as to the viability of the airborne division still persisted, particularly in the mind of General McNair. The status of the airborne division was still much in question and McNair had about come around to the view that no airborne unit larger than the battalion should be continued when in December the 11th Airborne Division engaged in a maneuver in the Carolinas. With McNair himself present as an observer, in company with Secretary of War Stimson, the 11th Airborne's commander, Major-General Joseph Swing, was sharply conscious of how much hinged on the outcome of the maneuver.

Making use of the new radar and pathfinder techniques, one serial after another of airplanes and gliders (the gliders for the first time in double tow) took to the air at night from four widely dispersed airfields. Almost unerringly they found their way to thirteen designated areas and dropped eighty-five per cent of the troops on target. Aircraft and gliders delivered a total of 12,282 men within a period of thirty-nine hours.

Although deficiencies were still apparent (what, for example, to do with glider pilots once they had brought in their gliders?), observers deemed the maneuver an unqualified success. General McNair was 'very pleased'. When a few weeks later the 17th Airborne Division staged a maneuver with similar success, McNair was at last convinced.

For the period of the Second World War, at least, the airborne division was in the United States Army to stay.

In Britain, meanwhile, formation of a second British airborne division – the 6th – had been slowed by the necessity to provide additional units and replacements for the 1st Airborne Division in North Africa, Sicily, and later, Italy. By the time of the invasion of Sicily, the 1st at last had all its units: three parachute brigades of three battalions each (1st, 4th, and 2nd, the last temporarily attached) and the 1st Air Landing Brigade (glider infantry). One of the parachute battalions, the 156th, had been formed from volunteers among British infantry units serving in India and had received most of its training in India. (The British also created a separate Gurkha parachute battalion and an Indian parachute brigade, while the Australians also formed an airborne

battalion but disbanded it before the men saw action.)

Following the difficult drops in Sicily, the 1st Airborne Division next saw action on 9th September 1943. Under the command of Major-General G F Hopkinson, the division went ashore from British warships in the Italian 'heel' at the port of Taranto to capitalize on Italian surrender and then fought through much of the rest of the month as regular infantry. Meanwhile, on the night of 14th September, one company parachuted onto the Dodecanese island of Cos but met no resistance. The waiting Italians had even spread straw to soften the landing zone.

To fill the ranks of the 6th Airborne Division, a British command lacking in manpower reserves in the meantime adopted the expedient of converting previously existing ground units into parachute battalions. Yet in every case individuals who chose not to make the conversion were allowed to transfer to other battalions of the line. Men of ground units converted to glider infantry were afforded no such option.

The commander of the 6th was Major-General Richard N Gale, who as a brigadier had headed the first British airborne brigade when it was originally formed late in 1941. Unlike the 1st Division, the 6th had only two

Static trainer

parachute brigades, one battalion of which was made up of Canadians. (The 1st Division eventually was to leave one of its brigades behind in Italy).

As the General Officer Commanding Airborne Troops, 'Boy' Browning, set out to train the new division, the old problem remained: lack of aircraft for practice jumps. Only late in 1943 was the problem alleviated with commitment of a portion of the US 9th Troop Carrier Command to assist. It was great, the British troopers reported, to jump with some respectability out of a door instead of through a hole in the floor. Early in 1944, with

the allotment of two troop carrier groups of the Royal Air Force – numbers 38 and 46 – the problem of sufficient troop carriers for British parachutists at last was solved. Able to lift an entire division at once, General Browning was elated.

Even as that acute problem was finally eased, an electric tension had begun to grip Britain. Allied strategic air forces were at the time – late winter and early spring of 1944 – embarked on a comprehensive program to drive enemy aircraft from the skies over France. Day after day ships arrived in the mouth of the Clyde to disgorge thousands of American troops, great stuffed duffel bags in hand, or to land tons upon tons of supplies and equipment, everything from locomotives to dental fillings. To even the most casual observer it was apparent that the time was approaching when Allied armies were to launch the climactic stroke against Hitler's Germany with a mammoth invasion across the Channel into France.

As part of the vast preparation for the invasion, a use for the parachute that had begun not long after the French defeat in 1940 grew in importance. With particular attention to France, where British armies might most logically hope to return to the Continent, the British early had begun to succor resistance movements in the occupied countries of Europe, to include parachuting supplies and agents. In respect to France, where an internal resistance could be expected to weaken the foe and even participate actively in the return to the Continent, the British had set up within a headquarters called the Special Operations Executive, a special French section to recruit and train agents, help organize the resistance, and feed back intelligence by clandestine radio.

The United States had joined the program early in 1943 under the aegis of a cloak-and-dagger outfit, the Office of Strategic Services. Together the two nations parachuted or otherwise delivered into France a total of 768 agents trained under their auspices and 868 others recruited by the man

Recruits learn to land

who had fled France to lead resistance outside the country, Charles de Gaulle.

Aside from agents and radio operators, the three Allied nations sent into France by parachute three-man teams called 'Jedburgh' after the place in Scotland where they were trained. Composed of one American, one Britisher, and one Frenchman, men of the Jedburgh, unlike agents, wore uniforms. That was primarily because some of them lacked facility in the French language; if captured in uniform, they could claim combatant status under international rules of warfare. Being uniformed, they usually operated in localities where the internal resistance had established a measure of control. Similarly, several American Special Operations Groups, composed of 374 officers and men, parachuted into France to fight with the resistance forces.

Despite a German program of repression heaped upon repression, terror upon terror, as Allied invasion of France neared a vast shadow army existed in France and other occupied countries, sustained primarily through the medium of the parachute. The shadow army in France was preparing, the Germans knew, to act in concert with the invaders, but the Germans were powerless to prevent it. None could say with any certainty the army's strength: perhaps 100,000, maybe 200,000; and because the Americans and British had other priorities, many lacked arms. Yet all were imbued with love of country, hatred of the Nazis, and the comforting knowledge that deliverance was coming.

Even after the start of the invasion, the British continued to employ an entire airborne regiment in support of the Belgian, Dutch, French, and Italian resistance movements. Called the Special Air Service Regiment, the troops usually operated in small increments on such assignments as cutting roads and railways. Portions of the two French airborne battalions formed in Britain also participated on occasion, as did a company each of Dutch and Belgian airborne troops.

From the first, those who planned for the invasion of France contemplated employing airborne troops,

The gliders after D-Day

including airborne participation in an emergency invasion scheduled for early fall of 1942 in the event of the Russian armies showing signs of imminent collapse. The emergency plan assumed that four US parachute battalions and one British parachute brigade would be available. A second plan that looked to invasion in the summer of 1943 assumed the availability of one British parachute brigade and eleven US parachute battalions, including one airborne division. The decision to invade North Africa, which led to further Allied commitment in Sicily and Italy, prompted cancellation of both plans.

A new plan, Operation Overlord, which pointed to invasion in late spring of 1944 and was approved by the Allied high command in the summer of 1943, was at first designed to employ portions of two airborne divisions – the British 6th and the US 101st – both because the British 1st and the US 82nd were at the time committed in the Mediterranean and because the number of troop carrier aircraft expected to be available was small. Through the actual invasion, the broad outlines of the original Plan Overlord remained constant: landings on the coast of Normandy between Le Havre and the base of the Cherbourg peninsula; but the original modest airborne commitment was

destined to be much enlarged.

The first plan gave priority to the British airborne to make possible quick seizure of the city of Caen and crossings over the Orne River on the British left flank, both with the object of speeding emergence into open country leading to Paris. Only one American parachute battalion was to be used at first, with the mission of eliminating a battery of coastal artillery on a cliff overlooking the American invasion beach, known as Omaha. If additional aircraft became available or if planes were able to fly additional missions, other American parachutists were to seize crossings over small streams inland from Omaha Beach.

By the time General Eisenhower, early in January 1944, arrived from the Mediterranean to become Supreme Allied Commander for Operation Overlord, both troop carrier planes and airborne units had increased. Available then were both the British airborne divisions and the American 82nd and 101st and enough aircraft to transport the bulk of three divisions. The addition of a second American invasion beach – Utah – to the west of Omaha prompted the planners to shift priority on airlift to the Americans. As finally determined, the 6th Airborne Division was to seize crossings over the Orne, secure the British left flank by holding a ridge northeast of Caen, and eliminate

Left: Indian-style war-paint for the invasion of Europe. *Above:* Hooked up ready for the jump

a battery of coastal guns at the village of Merville that was in a position to enfilade British invasion beaches. The 1st Airborne Division was to be available as an airborne reserve to be employed in the British beachhead if needed. The American divisions were to seize exits of causeways leading through marshland behind Utah Beach, block reinforcements moving against Utah Beach, gain crossings over the Merderet River that might be exploited for sealing off the Cherbourg peninsula, and later take the town of Carentan as a step in linking Omaha and Utah Beaches. The broad objective of both British and American airborne divisions thus was to protect the open flanks of the invasion forces.

As the planning continued, the US Army's Chief of Staff, General Marshall, deemed the concept for employment of the airborne divisions too conservative. To Eisenhower he suggested a plan developed by the Chief of the Army Air Forces, General Arnold: establishing an 'airhead' on D-Day more than fifty miles inland

close enough to Paris to threaten the French capital and crossings over the Seine river. Although Eisenhower studied the plan carefully, he rejected it. 'Mass in vertical envelopments is sound,' he wrote Marshall, 'but since this kind of an enveloping force is immobile on the ground, the collaborating force must be strategically and tactically mobile. So the time for the mass vertical envelopment is after the beachhead has been gained and a striking force built up.'

As the time for the invasion neared, neither of the founders of the Allied airborne forces was destined to participate. In October 1942, the Britisher, John Rock, had died in a glider accident. Although Bill Lee had come to England in command of the 101st Airborne Division, he incurred a heart attack in February 1944 that was to force his return to the United States. The 82nd Airborne Division's former artillery commander, Maxwell Taylor, moved over and up to command the 101st. At Taylor's urging, many of the American paratroopers entering Normandy on D-Day shouted their founder's name as they jumped: 'Bill Lee!'

The strength of the 82nd and 101st Airborne Divisions meanwhile had sharply increased, even though the Army Ground Forces commander, General McNair, rejected an overture by the 82nd's commander, Major-General Matthew B Ridgway, based on the experience in Sicily, to revise the airborne table of organization and equipment and almost double the 8,000 men in the divisions. Despite McNair's refusal, the two divisions accomplished much the same through *ad hoc* means. To each General Eisenhower attached a separate parachute regiment, and between them the two divisions split a separate glider infantry regiment, thus giving each three parachute infantry regiments and a three-battalion glider infantry regiment. Each also had two parachute artillery battalions (75mm pack howitzers) and a glider artillery battalion equipped with 105mm howitzers.

As in most previous airborne operations, the landings were to be made in darkness. Parachutists of both the British and the American divisions were to land first, preceded by pathfinders, whereupon glider reinforcements were to arrive just before dawn and again late in the day.

The pilots of the troop carrier aircraft were more experienced than those who had sown the troops broadcast in Sicily, but deficiencies still were apparent. They participated in several airborne maneuvers in England during the spring, but the demands for hauling air freight were still heavy and served to restrict the number of planes available for joint training. For the pilots, the constant shifting from air freight missions to day and night formation flying and back again was disconcerting.

Despite General Marshall's belief that the airborne plan was conservative, there were many – including General Eisenhower himself – who considered it downright risky. The commander of the Allied Expeditionary Air Force, Air Marshal Sir Trafford Leigh-Mallory, took an increasingly pessimistic view of what he called 'this very speculative operation'. A week before D-Day he told

General Eisenhower that he deemed it unwise to risk his troop carriers, that losses among them were likely to run over fifty per cent. Late intelligence showing that the Germans had recently moved an entire division in behind Utah Beach heightened the concern. Nor was confidence fostered by the discovery that in a book entitled 'Paratroops', published a few months earlier by a Czech officer working with the French in London, Major F O Miksche, the author discussed a hypothetical invasion of Normandy in terms of two of the drop zones Allied planners had actually chosen. Yet despite predictions that losses among the airborne troops might run as high as eighty per cent, General Eisenhower considered the airborne role so vital to the success of the invasion that if the invasion was to proceed, the airborne risks would have to be accepted.

Seaborne and airborne invasion forces come together as a bren-gun carrier crew encounters an abandoned glider

Concern over devastating losses was nevertheless heavy in many an Allied commander's mind – including Eisenhower's – when in the evening of 5th June 1944, British and American paratroopers made their way to waiting C-47s and converted Albemarle and Stirling bombers on airfields all over the south of England. One of the American troopers saw the final minutes this way: 'Small quiet groups sit under the plane wings and watch the sun go down. Eight o'clock. "It won't be long now," says Porter the medic. Porter the medic who was machine-gunned the next day and will never leave the cemetery in Ste Mère - Eglise. Nine o'clock. A few planes start to roar. Checking their motors. Jesus Christ, I hate that sound! Ten o'clock. Their nervousness increasing, the men get up and relieve themselves continuously. Ten-thirty. We clamber aboard the plane and sit down . . . This is the end of our training, this is the one-way road. I try to sleep, but I can't. Now the whole field is shaking with the roar of motors – the final warmup. Ten forty-five. "There they go!" the crew chief shouts. "They're off!" Eleven o'clock. Our tail swings around. We wheel about and head up the runway. Dead silence. I swallow my seasick pills and try to act nonchalant, but it's no go. My legs are weak and my throat is dry and I can only talk in a stuttering whisper. Some of the boys are chain-smoking their cigarettes. A few are asleep. With a soft rush, we leave the ground; we are airborne. There is no going back'.

Accompanying the British pathfinders was a small force of infantry and engineers flying in six gliders with the mission of executing a *coup de main* against two vital bridges spanning the Canal de Caen and the

Orne River between Caen and the sea. The lead glider landed only forty-seven yards from the canal bridge, and all the others except one came to earth nearby. Assembling swiftly, the British troops took both bridges after short but violent firefights with German sentries.

Contingents of a badly scattered parachute battalion of the 5th Parachute Brigade arrived a few hours later to help hold the bridge over the Canal de Caen – which would thereafter be known as the Pegasus Bridge – while another parachute battalion moved to help defend the bridge over the Orne. Shortly after noon, the men at the Pegasus Bridge picked up the wail of a bagpipe in the distance. At two o'clock the piper at the head of a band of Commandos led the way across the bridge. Although sniper fire was still striking the metal girders of the bridge, it was a moment of elation. British airborne and seaborne forces had linked.

The remaining battalion of the 5th Parachute Brigade meanwhile secured a town to the east barring access to the bridges and cleared anti-landing obstacles (long poles set into the ground at a slant) from high ground nearby. Two hours after the first parachutists jumped, gliders bearing an advance detachment of General Gale's division headquarters and the division's anti-tank guns landed with precision. Although snipers and small contingents of Germans – in one case supported by three tanks – harrassed the British troops through the rest of D-Day, no major threat against the vital bridges developed. Despite the loss of two Stirlings with their crews and passengers, casualties in the 5th Parachute Brigade were in general light.

The 3rd Parachute Brigade in the meantime had jumped to carry out its primary mission of eliminating the enemy's coastal guns at Merville and a secondary mission of destroying bridges over the Dives river to the east and southeast in order to inhibit movement of German reserves. Although all the battalions were badly scattered, in all cases enough men responded to the sound of hunting horns – the British airborne's way of signalling assembly – to accomplish the appointed tasks. All the bridges were destroyed on schedule, as was the formidable concrete-encased battery near Merville, the latter by a band of some 150 men under Lieutenant-Colonel T B H Otway, acting with an intrepidity nowhere exceeded on D-Day.

Scattered drops caused mainly by pilots taking evasive action against anti-aircraft fire sharply reduced the numbers who assembled in time to move against the battery. Otway and his courageous 150 nevertheless worked their way to barbed wire and minefields surrounding the position, there to lie in wait for three gliders that, after the manner of German gliders at Fort Eben Emael, were to land full astride the battery. The gliders never made it: one never left England because its tow rope broke; the two others, badly shot up by anti-aircraft fire, landed well away from the objective.

Even as the two gliders circled, German machine gunners newly awake to the presence of Colonel Otway and his parachutists opened a deadly fire. Setting off a demolition charge to create a gap through the wire and mines, the men charged forward. Some of them somehow made their way onto the battery, there to fight the Germans in hand-to-hand combat. They subdued the last defenders and spiked the guns only half an hour before naval gunners were scheduled to open fire in an effort to neutralize the battery in case the parachutists failed. Otway lost seventy men killed, wounded, or missing – almost half his force – but the guns of Merville would pose no threat to men coming ashore on the British beaches.

As darkness descended on D-Day and gliders bringing the 6th Airborne Division's airlanding brigade arrived, General Gale could point to all objectives achieved. Several of the parachute battalions already were moving onto high ground between the Orne and the Dives to start forging what was to become the airborne division's bridgehead over the Orne. For two months they were destined to hold there, protecting the flank of British

The gliders' tails have been detached for quick unloading

123

The Allies reach German soil. *Above:* Halifax tugs and Hamilcar gliders line up.
Below: Landings north of Hamminkeln

Above: British gliders near Hamminkeln. *Below:* American landing east of the Rhine.

and Canadian armies, then to participate in the explosion of the beachhead and the march to the Seine. From D-Day until the day they assembled for return to England, the airborne troops were in action for eighty-three days. In the process, they took 2,695 casualties.

If the scattered drop of the British airborne troops was serious, that of the American divisions was near catastrophic. Taking evasive action against a welter of anti-aircraft fire, unable to make out drop zones obscured by low clouds, the pilots scattered their loads all over the landscape, some sticks as far as twenty-five miles from the appointed spots. Hundreds of men plummeted into vast stretches of marshes that the Germans had flooded to augment their defenses; weighted down by their equipment, trapped in their harness, unknown numbers drowned. Many landed full on German positions, some almost atop headquarters of the 91st Infantry Division, which German commanders in response to Hitler's concern for landings in that part of Normandy had only recently moved to the area. Twenty men came down in or close to the town square of Ste Mère - Eglise, behind Utah Beach, where one man dangled in his harness for more than two hours from the church steeple, playing dead, until the Germans finally cut him down and captured him.

Here, there, everywhere, men played out thousands of intense individual dramas – sometimes living through them, sometimes not. Many a paratrooper held his breath time after time while snapping a toy metal cricket to identify himself. The response might be a reassuring two snaps from another American, or it might be a blast of German fire.

In the confusion men nevertheless got together in small groups, found leadership, and with the knowledge born of detailed pre-assault briefings, moved toward assigned objectives. The very fact of their dispersion had an effect, as it had in Sicily, on German reaction. Excited cries of '*Fallschirmjäger! Fallschirmjäger!* – some of them inspired by dummy paratroopers fused with firecrackers and dropped far afield – early began to pour into various German headquarters in such volume that for a long time it was impossible to fit the drops into a discernible pattern.

Hundreds of confused local combats were raging when shortly before dawn the drone of planes came again, followed by a strange fluttering of gliders brushing the air. Men in the plywood craft closed their eyes, locked arms, and steeled themselves for the inevitable crash landing. The gliders of the 101st Airborne Division for the most part made it to the vicinity of the appointed landing zones, though anti-landing obstacles and hedgerows of thick earth interlaced with trees and brush - a feature of that part of Normandy - took an inevitable toll. One of those killed in a crash was the assistant division commander, Brigadier-General Don Pratt. The gliders bringing men of the 82nd Airborne Division were even harder hit. Fewer than half made the correct landing zones, and most of the others crashed into hedgerows or buildings or carried their heavily laden occupants to watery deaths in the flooded marshes.

Few were the 75mm pack howitzers that survived the scattered parachute drops, or the 105s that emerged serviceable from the wrecked gliders. Fortunate it was that the airborne troops on occasion seized German artillery pieces and turned them to their advantage, but in the main it was a case of innumerable infantry skirmishes where fire support no more powerful than that from a salvaged 60 or 81mm mortar might make the difference between success or failure.

For all the near catastrophe of the drops and landings, the little bands that got together in the darkness somehow gained the more vital objectives. A battalion commander of the 101st with seventy-five men, including some from the 82nd, found that the guns of a coastal battery along the west flank of Utah Beach had been removed. With his seventy-five men and others that gradually trickled in, he secured one of the causeways from the beach and formed a blocking position to protect the flank of the landing beach. Another battalion commander gathered ninety men but was so delayed by German

Crumpled wings were a frequent mishap in glider landings

machine gun fire that he failed to reach another of the causeways until early afternoon, after seaborne troops had already fought their way through. Remnants of two battalions gained bridges over the Douve river and a lock that controlled the flow of the tide; the gains later might be exploited for a drive on Carentan to link Utah Beach with Omaha.

Bands of similar size to the 82nd Airborne Division in the meantime captured Ste Mère-Eglise, defended it against a small counterattack, blocked the main road from Cherbourg northwest of the town, and early the next day were to establish contact with the seaborne troops approaching from Utah Beach. Remnants of other battalions dropping west of the Merderet river, having come down on the edge of the assembly area of the enemy's 91st Division, experienced stiffer fights but nevertheless seized crossings over the Merderet, however beleaguered.

Despite these achievements, as night approached neither the commander of the 82nd Airborne Division, General Ridgway, nor the commander of the 101st, General Taylor, was in genuine control of his division. Only some 2,500 of 6,600 men of the 101st who had dropped during the early morning hours had gotten together; of the 82nd, even fewer. Yet the divisions would in the end tabulate their actual D-Day losses at 2,499 – a factor

of fifteen per cent as opposed to the eighty per cent some had predicted. More important, the weakness of the two divisions was for the moment balanced by the enemy's failure to organize concerted counterattacks, a failure in part attributable to the confusion generated by the very presence of the airborne troops. Furthermore, glider reinforcements were to arrive during the night, and contact with the seaborne invaders soon was to provide the lightly-armed paratroopers and glider infantry with tank, artillery, and naval gunfire support. The overall effect of the airborne landings behind Utah Beach, for all the dispersion, was to constitute a real and tangible contribution to the success of the invasion.

The airborne assault on D-Day was the largest the Allies had yet staged, and the number arriving on the first day exceeded the number of Germans who had come in with the first wave on Crete. Employing 2,435 aircraft and 867 gliders, the Allies had delivered almost 17,000 men to France by air within the first twenty-four hours. Forty-three aircraft and an untold number of gliders were lost. As with the British, the American airborne divisions were slow to depart the line: the 82nd thirty-two days after D-Day; the 101st, thirty-four.

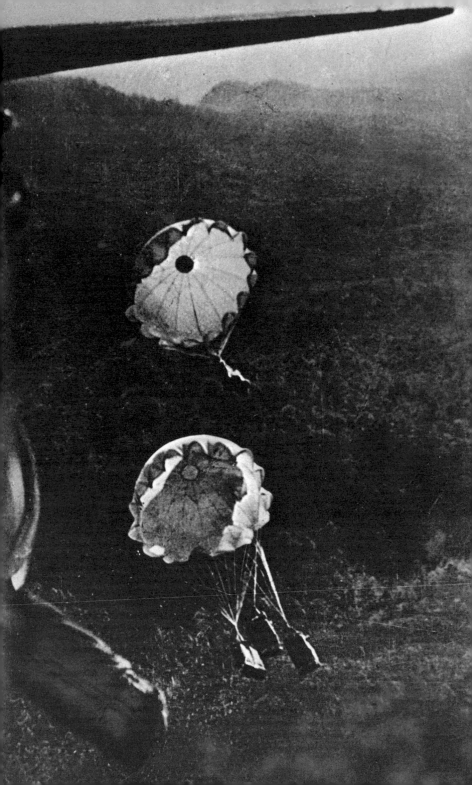

Towards a climax beyond the Rhine

On the basis of the experience in Normandy, both General Ridgway and General Taylor urged reorganizing the American airborne division. Since training directives and infantry doctrine were based on a triangular organization, the two-battalion glider infantry regiment, the two-platoon glider infantry company, and the parachute platoon composed of one machine gun and two rifle squads had forced commanders to improvise either new units or new tactics. Although the attachment of an additional glider infantry battalion and a separate parachute regiment to each division had alleviated some of the deficiencies, those were makeshift solutions. Furthermore, the effort to streamline the division by cutting down on transport and supporting services had come close to immobilizing it. General Taylor for his part also urged addition of a second glider field artillery battalion equipped with 105mm howitzers.

Although the War Department received the proposals sympathetically, concern about overall manpower requirements slowed response. Not for several months was any change to be forthcoming, so that the divisions would fight in Operation Market in September under the same makeshift augmentation as in Overlord.

While creating a new table of organization and equipment for the airborne division was out of the province of the theatre commander, establishing a central headquarters to improve coordination between airborne troops and troop carriers was not. Even before D-Day there had been some discussion about brigading all US and British airborne and troop carrier units under a central headquarters (General Browning, in particular, had espoused it). As General Eisenhower viewed the proposal, there should be an air force officer commanding the combined headquarters. While British and American troop carrier units functioned directly under the combined commander, the airborne troops should be attached to two corps headquarters: one American, one British.

Despite objections from some British officers who were wary lest the Royal Air Force use the precedent

Parachute drop of supplies to American troops operating on the edge of jungle terrain in New Guinea

for gaining control of airborne troops, the experience of another scattered drop in Normandy gave impetus to the proposal, and General Eisenhower's view prevailed. The commander of the combined headquarters, the Supreme Commander pointed out, would assume responsibility for joint training, developing technical equipment, planning airborne operations, and supplying airborne troops by air. The corps commanders, rather than the combined commander, would command the troops once they hit the ground, but the combined commander would be responsible for the logistical support until normal ground lines of communication were established.

To command the new headquarters, General Eisenhower chose the head of the Ninth Air Force, General Brereton. At the veteran airman's urging, the new headquarters, which became operational on 2nd August, was later renamed the First Allied Airborne Army. Under Brereton, in addition to the 9th Troop Carrier Command and such troop carrier formations of the Royal Air Force as might be allocated from time to time, was the British Airborne Corps (General Browning) and a similarly new American headquarters, the XVIII Airborne Corps, commanded by General Ridgway. General Gavin moved up to command the 82nd Airborne Division.

Since a projected second Allied invasion of France – landings on the French Riviera – was mounted from resources of the Mediterranean Theater rather than of General Eisenhower's command, the airborne operation planned to support the invasion had no connection with the

new First Allied Airborne Army. Planning took place within headquarters of the US Seventh Army, which created a provisional airborne division and a provisional troop carrier division from resources available to Field Marshal Sir Henry Maitland Wilson's Allied Force Headquarters in the Mediterranean. The commander of the airborne troops was Major-General Robert T Frederick, whose former command, the First Special Service Force (composed of American and Canadian volunteers) had been parachute-trained but in fighting in Italy had participated only in ground operations.

The provisional airborne division, later designated the First Airborne Task Force, included the British 2nd Independent Parachute Brigade under Brigadier C H V Pritchard, a unit the 1st Airborne Division had left behind when quitting Italy for England in order to afford the British in Italy an

airborne capability. As it turned out, the brigade had fought for seven months in the line as regular infantry and in the end mounted only one airborne operation in Italy: a drop of sixty men north of Rome late on 1st June 1944, in an effort to prevent German forces withdrawing to the northern Apennines from carrying out extensive demolitions.

American airborne units included the 509th Parachute Infantry Battalion that under another name had jumped in North Africa; the 1st Battalion, 551st Parachute Infantry, that had done some ground fighting in Italy but would be making its first combat jump; a separate parachute field artillery battalion and a separate glider infantry battalion; and the 517th Parachute Combat Team. Encompassing a parachute field artillery battalion, the latter had started out as a component of the 17th Airborne Division but had come overseas as a separate unit and was to experience its first combat action. In addition, the Americans contributed a number of small units – field artillery, antitank, engineers, signal, and the like – that were standard ground units given a hasty course in travelling by glider at a special school set up near Rome.

With a total strength of 9,742 men transported in 535 troop carrier aircraft and 465 gliders, the First Airborne Task Force was to land approximately fifteen miles inland in the vicinity of the town of Le Muy. The airborne troops were to seize Le Muy and other communications centers nearby in order to block German movements against landing beaches extending from St Tropez almost to Cannes.

Rising from ten airfields in Italy in the early darkness of 15th August, the airborne units made an uneventful flight across the Mediterranean, the pilots maintaining tight formation all the way. Only as the planes crossed the coastline did trouble develop in the form of a thick bank of fog. Few pilots were able to spot the lights set in place by preceding pathfinders (only three of nine pathfinder teams had reached the correct drop zones, in any case) and had to depend either on homing on the pathfinders' 'Eureka'

radar beacons or on calculating an estimated time in flight from airfield to target. Again Allied parachutists came down all over the landscape.

Fortunate it was that the Germans were far weaker in southern France than Allied intelligence had discerned (the German high command had already been contemplating withdrawal) and also that after dark the men and women of the French resistance practically controlled vast stretches of the countryside. Opposition nowhere took the form of anything more serious than occasional small-arms skirmishes.

Despite the scattered drop, all objectives were soon in hand, even though the fog delayed arrival of the 2nd Parachute Brigade's artillery and anti-tank pieces until late afternoon. Although the paratroopers tried to clear glider landing zones of anti-landing obstacles, many were still in place when the gliders arrived and wreaked considerable havoc among the frail craft. Most of the day's casualties were attributable less to enemy fire than to the hazards of the drops and landings: approximately 240 men killed or injured – mostly the latter.

One of the more spectacular events of the day was attributable to the scattered drop. Twenty-nine planes dumped some men of the 509th Parachute Infantry Battalion, two full batteries of parachute field artillery with their guns, and portions of two other batteries just inside the coastline, not far from St Tropez. After weathering the preliminary Allied naval bombardment, without casualties, the airborne troops captured a German anti-aircraft battery, two coastal batteries, and 240 Germans. When leading American ground troops entered St Tropez, they found the paratroopers attacking the last German strongpoint in the town.

Additional contact with the seaborne forces was established elsewhere before the day was out. When on the third day Hitler ordered the

Germans to pull out of southern France, American ground troops already had passed beyond the positions of the airborne troops.

Of the units making up the First Airborne Task Force, only the 2nd Parachute Brigade was destined to execute another airborne operation (though the 517th Parachute Combat Team was subsequently assigned to the US 13th Airborne Division). Returned quickly to Italy, General Pritchard's brigade began to prepare for German withdrawal from Greece, which appeared likely in view of Russian advances into the Balkans that soon might isolate the Germans in Greece. The airborne troops were to jump near Athens and gain control of the city in order to maintain order and forestall occupation by Greek guerrillas intent on civil war.

Jumping by day on 14th October 1944, the parachute brigade quickly established control in Athens. Upon arrival of seaborne reinforcements, units of the brigade fanned out to other portions of the country, but in the end British numbers proved too few to forestall bloody fighting by Greek against Greek.

For all the focus on large-scale airborne operations in Europe, several smaller operations had been taking place in the Pacific, plus one on the Asiatic mainland that constituted the only strategic Allied airborne operation of the war. The latter was Operation Thursday, which began on 5th March 1944, before D-Day in Europe, and was aimed at driving the Japanese from Burma and reopening a long segment of the Ledo Road as far as the town of Myitkyina, a major Japanese supply base. Although few parachutists participated, gliders were employed along with considerable airlanding of troops, supplies and equipment in maneuvers that may contain more lessons for the future than do the more conventional tactical airborne operations in Europe.

The Japanese drive through southeast Asia having stopped short of the Burmese border with India, British and Indian troops under Major-General Orde C Wingate had invaded northern Burma in March of 1943. So successful were Wingate's operations in rear of Japanese positions that the

Gliders abandoned after the landing near Hamminkeln

Allied Combined Chiefs of Staff directed expanding them. Unquestioned aerial superiority over the Japanese having been attained, aerial resupply in volume seldom known before appeared practical. When an Indian division became surrounded in an operation in southern Burma, American and British aircraft flew some 10,000 tons of supplies over towering mountains to enable the Indians to break out, thus proving in advance of Operation Thursday for any who still might have doubted, following Wingate's successes, that aerial resupply on a large scale in the jungles of Burma was feasible.

An American officer, Colonel Philip Cochran, was assigned to develop a special unit equipped with C-47 transport planes, liaison planes, gliders, fighter-bombers, and medium bombers. On Cochran's conglomerate unit, known as the First Air Commando Force, the success of Operation Thursday depended.

While Gurkha and West African troops under British command approached Myitkyina from the north and American and Chinese troops under Major-General Joseph W Stillwell came in from the west, the bulk of an Indian division was to move in gliders and C-47s some one hundred miles behind Japanese lines south of Myitkyina railway, and in general disrupt Japanese supply and movement of reserves to the north. Cochran's First Air Commando Force was to deliver the troops and vast tons of supplies and equipment to two natural clearings in the jungle.

At the last minute, aerial photographers revealed that the Japanese had obstructed one of the clearings, so that everything had to be directed toward the other, known as 'Broad-

En route to the dropping zone in southern France

way'. The first night thirty-seven gliders landed on Broadway*, eight others came down nearby, and nine went down near Japanese installations. Since some of the gliders crashlanded and obstructed the clearing, others had to be recalled. In the landings thirty men were killed and thirty-three injured, but 539 others and two bulldozers made it safely. The next night Broadway was again ready to receive gliders, along with another small clearing discovered nearby, and air strips at both places were soon prepared to receive C-47s. By the end of the first week, 9,052 men, 175 ponies, 1,183 mules, and more than 500,000 pounds of stores had been delivered to the two strips.

As the Indian division moved northward toward Myitkyina and as Stillwell's column, spearheaded by a special American force known as Merrill's Marauders, approached from the west, C-47s and even liaison planes, the latter sometimes evacuating casualties, kept both forces supplied. By parachute the airmen dropped engineering equipment, medical supplies, rations, and ammunition and sometimes dropped clothing and grain in free fall from an altitude of about 150 feet.

As Wingate's Indian troops moved out from Broadway, a third Indian brigade soon joined them after an overland march. Wingate himself was killed on the 13th in a plane crash, ten days before his troops opened another advanced air strip to receive a fifth brigade.

Merrill's Marauders were the first to reach the air strip at Myitkyina, arriving undetected on 17th May, whereupon a Chinese regiment quickly seized the strip. Five hours later gliders brought in airborne engineers and their equipment. Before the day was ended, transport planes were landing despite Japanese artillery fire. Not for ten more weeks would the Japanese withdraw from Myitkyina itself, but all the while the airlift operated, mainly at night and often under artillery fire, proving the

* *Chindit* by Brigadier Michael Calvert D S O who commanded the Broadway force, will be published later in this series.

ability of Allied forces to bring in vast tons of supplies and thousands of reinforcements by air, an essential prerequisite to operations conducted with such size and speed in such inhospitable terrain.

American forces meanwhile were conducting a more conventional airborne operation when on 3rd and 4th July, the 503rd Parachute Infantry (less one of its battalions) parachuted onto an airstrip on Noemfoor Island off the coast of New Guinea in support of a seaborne landing made the previous day, another step in the Allied island-hopping campaign leading toward the Philippines and, eventually, the Japanese home islands. To the embarrassment of the paratroopers, they found engineers of the seaborne force waiting on the airstrip to greet them.

It was in some ways surprising that so few airborne operations were conducted in the Pacific, since the island-hopping nature of the Allied campaign would appear to lend itself admirably to the capabilities of airborne troops. The small number was attributable to no shortage of airborne troops, for in addition to the 503rd Parachute Infantry, which had long been present, General Swing's 11th Airborne Division arrived in the Pacific in the summer of 1944, only to be used on Leyte in the Philippines in a conventional ground role. (On 4th December, a lone C-47 dropped men and guns of a 75mm artillery battery on a ridge to provide fire support for a ground attack, the only American use of parachutists on Leyte.)

The answer lay in the composition of Allied forces in the Pacific: as the Allied offensive grew, there were multitudes of landing craft for amphibious attacks and sufficient shipping to keep ground forces supplied, whereas troop carrier aircraft were limited and were vitally needed to supply widely deployed air force units. The constant diversion of troop carrier planes to supply missions showed plainly in the drop on Noemfoor Island, where even in the face of no opposition, the pilots scattered the paratroopers widely. In the wake of that experience, air leaders set up a training program to re-educate pilots in formation flying, but so persistent

were the demands for air delivery of supplies that only one squadron at a time could be spared for training.

As a next step after Leyte, General Douglas MacArthur nevertheless proposed a regimental-sized airborne operation in conjunction with amphibious assaults on the main Philippine island of Luzon and a drive on the capital of Manila. To supplement a major drive on Manila from the north, the two glider infantry regiments of the 11th Airborne Division (all US airborne divisions except the 82nd and 101st had retained the early organization) were to land by sea on the shores of Nasugbu Bay southeast of Manila on 28th January 1945. Five days later the division's 511th Parachute Infantry was to help speed the advance northward on Manila by dropping astride the most prominent terrain feature in the area, the Tagaytay ridge.

So weak was Japanese opposition to the amphibious landings and the ground advance of the glider infantry that the airborne operation actually served little purpose other than to afford a convenient way of getting the paratroopers into the fight. Although the first serial of eighteen C-47s dropped about 345 troops correctly onto the undefended ridge, troopers in the next serial of thirty planes mistakenly took their cue to jump from a bundle of supplies that fell from one of the planes. Most of the men in a succeeding serial of fifty-one planes saw the collapsed 'chutes of their predecessors and also jumped too soon. Some 1,325 men were scattered from four to six miles away from the correct drop zone.

In the next airborne attack in the Philippines, sentiment to take the objective swiftly and dramatically had much to do with the choice of a combined airborne and amphibious assault. The objective was 'The Rock' – the island of Corregidor in Manila Bay – known to two generations of American soldiers before the Second World War and symbol of American dishonor in the loss of the Philippines.

Shaped like a tadpole, Corregidor is but three and a half miles long and

Across the Rhine – the landing in progress

139

American troops take up defensive positions after an eventful landing near Wessel, in Germany

one and a half miles across at its widest point, and much of the shoreline is steep, precipitous cliff. Despite the limited size of the target and the danger of parachutists dropping into the sea, American planners believed the Japanese would be so surprised by an airborne assault that it was worth the risks involved. The decision to use parachutists also drew some impetus from an intelligence estimate that only 850 Japanese were on the island, when actually there were over 5,000.

Although the best drop zone appeared to be an abandoned airfield on the 'tail' of the tadpole, men landing there would be exposed to plunging fire from higher ground on the 'head', so that the planners chose instead to put the men down on a former parade ground and golf course on the 'head'. Surrounded by destroyed prewar barracks, officers' homes, and headquarters buildings, the parade ground and golf course to-

gether afforded a drop zone less than half a mile long and about a quarter-mile wide, dangerously close to the precipitous cliffs.

Given those conditions, correlating such factors as wind direction and velocity and speed of the aircraft was vital. Since no plane would be over the drop zone longer than six seconds, each would have to make two or three passes, dropping six to eight paratroopers each time. It would take at least an hour to drop the first serial of a thousand men, and not until five hours later could a second serial be deposited. The planners themselves were prepared to accept a jump casualty rate of twenty per cent; the commander of the 503rd Parachute Infantry making the assault, Colonel George M Jones, predicted losses of fifty per cent.

Planes of the US Fifth Air Force bombarded Corregidor for several weeks preceding the assault, then on the morning of 16th February 1945, delivered a final blasting. American ships gave the island a three-day shelling.

Drop casualties in the first serial

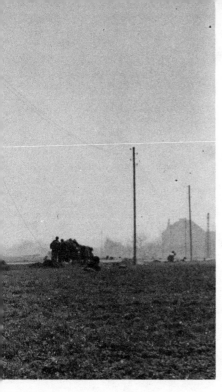

Japanese losses numbered at least 5,000, of which only twenty were captured.

At a simple flag-raising ceremony attended by General MacArthur, the airborne commander, Colonel Jones, saluted smartly and with words belying the difficulty of the fight, turned over the island. 'Sir', he said, 'I present to you Fortress Corregidor'.

Even before victory came in Europe, the war in the Pacific was moving toward an end faster than most observers recognized, and with it the prospect of further airborne operations. On the day after the Corregidor drop, on 17th February, a company of the 11th Airborne Division parachuted as part of a successful *coup de main* to rescue Allied prisoners held in a notorious Los Banos Camp near Manila. Although the 503rd Parachute Infantry was scheduled to jump on Negros Island in the Visayan group of the Philippines in late March 1945, lack of resistance to seaborne invasion prompted cancellation. Then on 2nd May, Gurkha troops numbering 800 parachuted to assist in capturing Rangoon, Burma. Whereupon, the final airborne assault by a battalion of the 11th Airborne Division's 511th Parachute Infantry, reinforced by a battery of parachute field artillery, turned out to be something of a farce. Jumping on 23rd June in an effort to block a suspected Japanese retreat through the Cagayan valley of northern Luzon, and employing seven gliders in the first and only use of gliders in the Pacific other than on the Asian mainland, the paratroopers found US ground troops on the drop zone to welcome them.

In Europe, in the meantime, the Allies had staged Operation Market, the war's largest airborne assault, and on 23rd December 1944, twenty men jumped as pathfinders to mark drop zones for aerial resupply of the encircled 101st Airborne Division at Bastogne in the Belgian Ardennes. (Ironically, fighting as regular infantry, the 101st at Bastogne probably achieved its finest hour). Although a number of other airborne operations were to be proposed, particularly by airmen and airborne enthusiasts who wanted to see the airborne forces tested in a truly strategic role, only

were high – twenty-five per cent – but the assault succeeded beyond all expectations. Held under cover by air and sea bombardment, the Japanese directed little small-arms fire at the paratroopers or anti-aircraft fire at the planes, and none of the parachutists fell into the sea. The first serial swiftly secured the drop zones and two hours later delivered supporting fire to help an infantry battalion come ashore in landing craft.

Lest alerted Japanese defenders invoke their wrath on the next serial of paratroopers, Colonel Jones gained approval for the rest of his regiment to come in by boat. As the fight for Corregidor lapsed into a large-scale mop-up, the only other use of air was for dropping supplies.

The mop-up turned into one of the war's grimmest operations. Not until 2nd March had it progressed to a point that American commanders deemed the island basically secure. Even then numbers of diehard Japanese remained to be rooted out. Over a thousand Americans were killed, wounded, and missing.

Awaiting the order to move. Paratroops of the 1st Airborne Task Force

one more airborne assault remained. Whether that one was necessary or even warranted under the circumstances would forever remain conjecture.

The operation was Varsity, an assault on 24th March 1945, by a division each of British and Americans in the vicinity of the little German city of Wesel to help Field-Marshal Montgomery's 21st Army Group across the Rhine River. By the time Montgomery's elaborate preparations were completed (they rivaled D-Day in complexity and numbers), an American army had already jumped the Rhine on a bridge seized intact at Remagen and another crossed the night before Montgomery's assault without so much as an artillery preparation.

Although the Germans concentrated such forces as they could muster in the vicinity of Wesel, the German Army at that stage of the war had few resources left. It was, one German Chief of Staff noted, a 'shadow of an army', morale of the troops varying 'from suspicion to callous resignation', an officer corps which 'lacked confidence and wondered just what were the demands of duty'. It was, he said, an army that 'could only pretend to resist'.

Sorely beset with manpower problems, the British were slow to reconstitute the 1st Airborne Division after the heavy losses incurred in Operation Market. That left the British assignment to the 6th Airborne Division, out of the line since the preceding August and commanded by Major-General E Bols, who assumed command when General Gale moved up to become deputy commander of the First Allied Airborne Army. On the American side, both the 82nd and 101st Airborne Divisions had fought long and hard as ground troops during the enemy's Ardennes counter offensive. So had the 17th Airborne Division, rushed from England during the counter offensive and committed in a regular infantry role; but with an eye to a crossing of the Rhine, General Eisenhower had pulled out the 17th at the first opportunity. The American assignment in the Rhine crossing fell to that division, commanded by Major-General William M

Miley, who as a major long months before had commanded the first parachute battalion formed in the United States.

As Miley and his command prepared to participate in the assault, the War Department came through with the long discussed reorganization of the American airborne division, to be effective on 1st March. Fulfilling, in general, the recommendations made earlier by Generals Ridgway and Taylor, the new table of organization increased the strength in parachute platoons and glider companies and added a third battalion to the glider infantry regiment. It also made standard the ratio of two parachute infantry regiments to one glider infantry regiment, so that one battalion of one of the 17th's glider infantry regiments had to disbanded and its men absorbed elsewhere. To constitute its second parachute regiment, the division received the 507th Parachute Infantry, which had fought as an attachment on D-Day to the 82nd Airborne Division. Other adjustments had to be made in the divisional artillery to afford two parachute artillery battalions and two glider battalions, both the latter equipped with 105s. The men also had to learn to operate two previously untried weapons – the 57 and 75mm recoilless rifles, weapons that were revolutionary in light weight and lack of recoil and would go a long way toward answering a chronic lack of effective anti-tank weapons in the airborne division.

As in Operation Market, General Brereton's First Allied Airborne Army was responsible for pre-assault training and planning for Operation Varsity. Command once the troops hit the ground was to pass to General Ridgway and the XVIII Airborne Corps.

Wesel with its road and rail network was an obvious focus for any attempt to cross the Rhine in Field-Marshal Montgomery's sector. Thus the assignment given the XVIII Airborne Corps was logical: to seize high ground crowned by a wood, the Diersfordter Wald, northwest of Wesel, thereby denying the enemy dominant observation on the river crossing sites, and to capture bridges over

Above: Some of the 1,500-plus planes and gliders lifting from England. *Below and right:* Advance through enemy territory

waterways north and northeast of Wesel, thereby blocking enemy movements and preparing the way for expanding the bridgehead.

Those were concentrated objectives admirably suited to the capabilities of two airborne divisions. At the same time, the closest objective, the Diersfordter Wald, was little more than a mile from the projected Rhine crossing sites. While that augured well for early link-up with the ground forces, it meant that if the airborne troops jumped before or coincident with the river assault, the ground troops would have to forego all but the shallowest preliminary artillery bombardment. Furthermore, the ground troops needed to begin their attack in darkness, whereas the experience in Market had shown daylight best for an airborne attack.

The Second Army commander, General Dempsey, suggested the solution – the river assault to take place the night of 23rd March, the airborne assault the next morning. However simple that might sound in retrospect, it was at the time a bold departure from previous experience.

A mammoth amphibious assault had already achieved considerable success when shortly before nine o'clock on the morning of 24th March, the steady drone of hundreds of airplane motors began to emerge from the west. For two hours and thirty-two minutes the deep, throbbing, bass hum of motors persisted. A great train composed of 889 escorting fighter planes, 1,696 transport planes, and 1,348 gliders (many in double tow) brought to the battlefield 21,680 paratroopers and glidermen, the most ever delivered in one foray. Following closely were 240 Liberator bombers dropping 582 tons of supplies, while another 2,153 fighter aircraft either maintained a protective umbrella over the target area or ranged far over Germany in quest of any German planes that might seek to interfere. In addition, 2,596 heavy bombers and 821 medium bombers attacked airfields, bridges, rail marshaling areas, and other targets throughout Germany. It was an awesome display of power.

Among the transport aircraft was the first plane specifically designed

with airborne troops in mind – the American C-46 Commando. Considerably larger than the C-47, the plane had a door on each side of the fuselage, which not only facilitated loading and unloading cargo but enabled two groups of paratroopers to jump at once. More men in one plane and jumping at the same time sharply cut down on dispersal.

Since a Rhine crossing somewhere near Wesel was so obviously coming and since the Germans were steeped in Montgomery's thorough and deliberate methods, the big worry in Operation Varsity was enemy anti-aircraft fire. The Germans did, in fact, expect an airborne assault, although they thought it would hit some ten miles northeast of Wesel to facilitate breaking out of the bridgehead. With that in mind, they had shifted as many mobile anti-aircraft pieces to the general area as they could muster. When Radio Berlin boasted that the Germans knew the paratroopers were coming, many took that to mean someone had betrayed the plan, but it was logicality rather than betrayal.

The sky was clear and bright in mid-morning of 24th March, but a ground haze aggravated by drifting smoke from a screen being maintained to protect the troops crossing the river lowered visibility close to the ground, though not enough to interfere with the drop. The first men to jump, a battalion of the 507th Parachute Infantry (the regimental commander, Edson Raff, had commanded America's first airborne assault in North Africa), received little anti-aircraft fire, probably because the flight arrived close behind attacks on the enemy's guns by fighter-bombers and artillery.

The paratroopers and gliders that followed, including gliders of the 6th Airborne Division preceding the British paratroopers, were not so lucky. Anti-aircraft fire was in some cases devastating. Landing full upon the headquarters and support elements of a German corps and division, the men also came under heavy small-arms fire on the drop and landing zones. Among those killed was the

Men of the 17th Airborne Division enter a C-46 in England which will carry them east of the Rhine

First Allied Airborne troops, prepared for opposition, move off from their gliders

A sharp-shooting sniper gave Thomas J Barnes of the 503rd a close shave shortly after the landing on Corregidor

commander of the 1st Canadian Parachute Battalion, Lieutenant-Colonel J S Nicklin, whose parachute caught in a tree, making him an easy target. Numbers of key men in all units were lost – either killed or wounded – including all officers of one battery of American parachute field artillery.

Although the American parachute drops were in some cases a mile or so off target, almost all drops and landings were compact, so that despite the enemy fire, the survivors quickly assembled and marched on their objectives. The resistance once the men were on the ground rapidly disintegrated. British and American parachutists shared capture of the Diersfordter Wald, British glider infantry took the town of Hamminkeln to block approaches to Wesel from the north, British parachutists quickly seized key bridges over the Issel river east and northeast of Hamminkeln,

17th Airborne Division counted 2,000 prisoners; the 6th Airborne Division, 1,500. By late afternoon supplies were moving across the Rhine in amphibious craft in such volume as to eliminate the need for additional supply by air.

A question remained nevertheless whether in terms of casualties, lost aircraft, and the depleted state of the enemy, Varsity was justified. During the first day, the 6th Airborne Division lost 347 men killed and 731 wounded, while the 17th Airborne lost 159 killed and 522 wounded. (Of over 1,000 men in the two divisions listed as missing, most quickly rejoined their units). The crews of American troop carriers alone lost 41 men killed, 163 missing, and 153 wounded. Over 80 gliders and 44 transport aircraft were destroyed and 623 damaged. Also lost were 15 B-24 Liberators flying aerial resupply missions.

While the figures might compare fairly favorably with first-day losses in previous airborne assaults, they would bear no comparison with the casualties of the ground troops who jumped the Rhine by amphibious assault. Between them, two American infantry divisions, for example, lost but 41 men killed, 450 wounded, and 7 missing. Nor did participation by paratroopers and glidermen provide appreciably more depth to the bridgehead at Wesel than that achieved at another point without airborne support.

Indeed, whether the entire massive effort that Field-Marshal Montgomery mounted for crossing the Rhine was either necessary or justified at that stage of the war was open to serious question. Yet in the jubilation of success that accompanied the operation, few but the most carping critics would labor the point.

'My dear General,' Prime Minister Churchill had said to General Eisenhower as the two watched the spectacular airborne assault from the west bank of the Rhine, 'the German is whipped. We've got him. He is all through.'

To a man and to a nation that, almost five long years before, had known the nadir of Dunkirk, the pyrotechnics of 24th March were sweet and just and good and right.

and American glider infantry and paratroopers took other bridges over the Issel river and the Issel canal closer to Wesel. As night approached, contact with British ground troops in Wesel was firm.

Operation Varsity was unquestionably a marked success. Within three hours after the first serials arrived over the area, all airborne troops were on the ground, along with 109 tons of ammunition, 695 vehicles, and 113 artillery pieces, and within a few hours all objectives were in hand. The

Whither the airborne

As Operation Varsity took place, General Brereton and his staff of the First Allied Airborne Army were continuing to search for an opportunity to launch a genuinely strategic airborne operation. They thought they had found it in Operation Arena. a proposal to land six to ten divisions by parachute, glider, and plane in the vicinity of Kassel, more than a hundred miles beyond the Rhine, as Allied armies broke out from their Rhine River bridgeheads. Once the airborne troops had established an airhead, ground divisions were to land by transport plane and seize high ground at the eastern edge of the Ruhr industrial district, thereby assisting a swift envelopment of the Ruhr. Planning went so far as to describe a target date of 1st May before General Eisenhower's headquarters disapproved. The armies on the ground were advancing so rapidly that they needed no help from the airborne. Another projected airborne assault, a plan to seize control of Berlin should German resistance suddenly collapse, also never came off.

The Second World War thus was to end with a record of only two strategic airborne operations: Crete and Burma, although the latter was not, in the strictest terms, a true airborne operation.

The objective of most of the airborne attacks was tactical, primarily to seize, hold, or otherwise exploit important tactical objectives to assist the advance of ground or seaborne forces. That was the Japanese goal in the limited operations in the Pacific; the German goal in Norway, the Netherlands, and at Fort Eben Emael and Salonika; the Russian goal at Vyazma and the Dnieper; the Allied goal in Sicily, Nadzab, Normandy, Noemfoor Island, southern France, the Netherlands, Tagaytay Ridge, Corregidor, Wesel, and Rangoon. In almost all those operations the airborne troops had a secondary mission of blocking or delaying enemy reserves.

Those were the objectives of another operation that failed to materialize: a drop by two US airborne divisions to assist the US Seventh Army across the Rhine. The army commander, Lieutenant - General Alexander M Patch, finally decided that he could gain his bridgehead at less cost with a quick surprise amphibious assault rather than to wait the week or ten days that would be necessary for the airborne divisions to get ready.

Other operations were directed specifically at halting enemy movement or trapping enemy forces: the German drop at Corinth, for example, and in the Ardennes; the American drop at Avellino; the small British jump north of Rome; the final American operation on Luzon. Although the Allies planned several such operations during the German withdrawal from France in the summer of 1944, in all cases ground

A canopy blooms, showing the hazard of landing in a strong breeze

troops reached the objectives first, which meant either that objectives were not being selected deep enough in enemy territory or that the airborne troops were taking too long to prepare. The last operation planned in Europe had a similar goal: the US 13th Airborne Division was to drop southeast of Stuttgart in April 1945, to block enemy escape from the city, but ground troops got to the objective first. That doomed the 13th Airborne Division – commanded by Major-General Eldridge G Chapman, who had originally commanded America's first airlanding battalion – to the dubious distinction of being one of only two US divisions to see no combat in the Second World War and the only Allied division in the European Theater not to be committed.

A number of operations were designed specifically to take airfields: the Germans in Norway, the Netherlands, and Crete; the Russians in several instances; several American and British drops in North Africa; the Americans at Nadzab and Noemfoor Island; the British at Athens. Some aimed at other small, specific objectives: the Italians on the island of Cepholonia; the Germans on Leros; the British on Cos. Some were no more than raids: the British in Apulia, at Brunéval, and in quest of the German heavy water plant in Norway; the Americans in eastern Tunisia; the German rescue of Mussolini; two Japanese operations on Leyte; and the Americans at the Los Banos Camp near Manila.

Particularly in France and Russia and to a lesser extent elsewhere in Europe and in Asia, special airborne units assisted internal resistance forces, and in the Vercors, the Germans employed glider troops to help fight the resistance. In the reinforcing drops in Sicily and the Salerno beachhead, the goal was to assist hard-pressed seaborne forces, while pathfinders dropped at Bastogne as a preliminary step to providing aerial supply to an encircled force.

Aside from a strategic role to create

an airhead far behind enemy lines, either the Western Allies, the Russians, or their adversaries thus used airborne troops for almost all conceivable missions commensurate with the state of air transport at the time. Burma, for example, can be said to have been an attempt to capture enemy command installations or otherwise to paralyze the enemy's system of command, communications, and supply, though no other operations were launched with that specific objective in mind. The early German operations can be said to have had at least the side effect of creating confusion and disorder among both civil and military personnel.

Although both American and British doctrine prescribed that airborne troops were to be removed from the battle soon after link-up with ground or seaborne forces, the practice often was tragically otherwise. The practice demonstrated a hazard, if not a shortcoming, of all elite forces: once they are committed, or are even available, hard-pressed ground commanders are tempted to use them as regular ground forces and are loath to give them up. The list of doctrinal violations is long: the British 1st Parachute Brigade and Colonel Raff's American battalion in North Africa; the 1st Airborne Division and subsequently the 2nd Independent Parachute Brigade in Italy; the First Special Service Force and the 504th Parachute Infantry in the Anzio beachhead; the 6th, 82nd, and 101st Airborne Divisions in Normandy; the 82nd and 101st after Operation Market; the 17th, 82nd, and 101st in the Ardennes; the 503rd Parachute Infantry on Corregidor; and the 11th Airborne Division throughout the Philippines campaign. Most of the casualties in the airborne units were incurred during those lengthy commitments as ground troops.

It was a situation shared by British Commandos and US Rangers, yet it was a serious development nevertheless. Why expend long, costly hours on specialized training and equipment, then expose the men to high losses in regular roles? Why enable men to volunteer and serve, perhaps, as privates in elite forces when the same men might perform a more valuable function as non-commission-ed officers in less elite company.

That is not to say that in time of true emergency elite units should not be employed for tasks other than those for which they were specifically trained. Being light outfits, capable of moving quickly, the 1st Airborne Division at Taranto and the 17th, 82nd, and 101st Airborne Divisions in the Ardennes were admirably suited for swift commitment at times when speed was vital. Yet the fact remains that 2,000 casualties in an elite force is a more serious matter than 2,000 casualties in a regular unit, where losses can be replaced at less cost in time and equipment. As even the United States, with its vast reservoir of manpower, found out, the pipeline providing elite volunteers eventually runs dry.

Perhaps the most serious problem faced by all the airborne troops during the Second World War – Russians, Germans, and Japanese included – was the shortage of troop carrier aircraft and adequately trained pilots. It was basically a question of priorities, and seldom were the airborne forces favoured. Deficiencies in Allied pilot training were understandable in early stages of the war – North Africa, for example, and Sicily – but even later, when adequate numbers of pilots and planes at last were available, the demands on the pilots to haul air freight seriously interfered with combined training and contributed directly to the dispersion prevalent in many an operation.

The Americans, for their part, never solved the problem of what to do with glider pilots once they had landed their gliders. The British gave their pilots rudimentary ground training, and upon landing, the pilots assembled as a ground unit capable of handling basic tasks. American glider pilots either had to attach themselves to a ground unit on their own volition or else wander the battlefield aimlessly until contact with ground troops was established.

Another problem lay in a marked inability of airborne troops to meet enemy tanks on anything like equal terms. The towed American 57mm anti-tank gun and the British equivalent, the 6-pounder, were highly vulnerable because of their lack of mobility, and both had to rely on fairly lucky hits at close range if they were to have any effect against such tanks as the Panther (Mark V) and Tiger (Mark VI). The individual anti-tank weapons – the American bazooka and the British PIAT – were effective if the user succeeded in getting close enough and hitting a vulnerable spot, but they were more emergency weapons than a genuine defense against armor. Otherwise, airborne troops had to depend upon artillery and the fighter-bomber, which are imperfect anti-tank weapons at best. Given the state of airborne science at the time, the best anti-tank weapon – another tank of comparable size and firepower – could not be brought to the battlefield by air. Only against the British at Arnhem did the Germans employ tanks in appreciable numbers against Allied airborne troops before ground contact was established, but the results in that case were disastrous. Indeed, the threat of enemy armor was one of the main arguments against a strategic airborne operation in Europe.

Although the shift from night to daylight attack paid off handsomely in Operation Market, the losses to anti-aircraft fire in Varsity – where total surprise was not present – revealed that daylight might not be the answer. Except for the problems with Allied anti-aircraft guns off Sicily, all the major night operations might have had less dispersion had troop carrier pilots been better trained and had more sophisticated pathfinder equipment been available. On the other hand, anti-aircraft batteries controlled by radar would incur small disadvantage from darkness, whereas fighter-bombers and artillery might execute a more effective counter-flak program in daylight. Surely the problem of assembly after landing is eased by day. The best that could be said was that the experience of the Second World War left the question of night versus daylight airborne attack unresolved.

As impressive in number, size, and accomplishment as were the airborne attacks of the Second World War, only the one fully independent airborne attack – Crete – can be said to have been decisive. That inevitably raises the question whether airborne troops were essential to the arsenal of the modern army or whether they were a luxury.

The German airborne attacks in Norway and the Netherlands were psychologically debilitating to the victims and obviously sped German success, but so superior were German ground forces that the same goals could have been achieved in only slightly less time by conventional means. In all cases ground or seaborne troops sealed the victory.

The airborne assault in Sicily spread confusion in German ranks and may have delayed a German counterattack against a segment of the American beachhead, but despite General Student's opinion, it is impossible to conclude that without airborne support, the amphibious assaults would have failed. However dramatic the reinforcing of the American beachhead at Salerno with airborne troops, the forces already in the beachhead had defeated the German counterattack that prompted the airborne reinforcement several hours before the first airborne troops arrived.

None of the Japanese airborne attacks was in any sense decisive, or even important. Even though the Allied use of airborne troops in Burma contributed to the capture of Myitkyina, the successful conclusion of the campaign owed more to the landing of conventional troops by transports on the Myitkyina airfield after it had been taken by ground troops.

Airborne troops dropping near Caen and behind Utah Beach made significant contributions to the success of D-Day in Normandy, particularly at Utah, where airborne troops prevented a reserve German division from reinforcing the beach defenders. Yet despite a lack of airborne support behind three other of the invasion beaches – including Omaha, where German defense was strongest – the amphibious forces landed successfully. The relative ease of the invasion of southern France left no question but that the invasion would have succeeded without airborne support. In the Pacific hardly any of the many successful amphibious assaults had airborne support, though that is not to say that the assaults might not have been facilitated by the use of airborne troops. Certainly the airborne drop on Corregidor eased the subsequent amphibious invasion, even though it is impossible to concede that without the airborne troops the invasion would have failed.

Operation Market came close to attaining a crossing of the Rhine that conceivably might have had far-reaching results. It actually made a valuable contribution in securing bridges over the Maas and Waal rivers. Yet it failed to achieve the primary objective for which it was designed – placing British ground troops in a position to outflank the Westwall and drive onto the North German Plain – and for which the high costs would have been acceptable. Nor can it be said that Operation Varsity was in any way essential for a successful British crossing of the Rhine.

The conclusion is inescapable that airborne forces as employed in the Second World War were a luxury – spectacular, impressive, and often highly useful, as many a luxury can be, but a luxury nevertheless. The expense of training specialized airborne troops, the diversion of resources from other programs, the leadership denied regular units by the diversion of highly qualified and motivated men into elite units, and the cost of providing special equipment such as planes, gliders, parachutes – all those would have to be weighed against the results.

Even the oft-expressed contention that by their very existence airborne troops forced the enemy to disperse his resources and his reserves to protect vital installations cannot be supported. Only in two instances – locating a division behind what became Utah Beach and shifting anti-aircraft units to oppose what became Operation Varsity – did the Germans prepare specifically against airborne attack. Much the same was true among Allies and Japanese in the Pacific and the Far East, and the Germans in Russia formed their defense of rear installations less against the threat of airborne attack than against partisans.

On the other hand, the fact that airborne troops turned out to be a luxury may have resulted from the way Allied commanders employed the new resource. A genuinely strategic instead of a tactical approach to the use of airborne troops might have produced decisive results. As it was, ground or other air actions, including strategic bombing and aerial resupply of ground troops, usually had priority, and ground commanders were reluctant to agree to an airborne attack unless they were sure it would not divert resources from more conventional operations. A reverse approach, looking upon airborne troops as something more than ancillary, might have contributed far more to the ultimate victory.

Since the Second World War, the Americans have launched three major airborne operations – two in Korea and one in Vietnam. Yet in both cases the operations appear to have been mounted more because the troops were available than because their use as parachutists was essential or even specifically needed. Under the particular conditions present in Vietnam, where the enemy lacks highly sophisticated anti-aircraft weapons, the helicopter assault took the place of the airborne assault. Whether a similar situation would prevail under other conditions is impossible to assess, or indeed whether with increasingly sophisticated anti-aircraft capability, airborne troops can be employed at all.

Yet to dismiss a development as revolutionary as the airborne on such a premise is to disregard man's oft-demonstrated ability to overcome almost any obstacle. Although the glider with its record of high casualties in landing was abandoned after the Second World War, would not a glider equipped with a motor retain the advantage of the glider's silent approach while providing the pilot an alternative to a crash landing? Might airborne troops be dropped in pressurized containers from planes – such as the American B-52 – that fly so high they are beyond sight or sound?

If Benjamin Franklin in 1784 could anticipate the kind of airborne operations that occurred during the Second World War, who is to say in 1970 but that even more spectacular airborne developments may not come to pass?

Bibliography

The author wishes to express his grateful acknowledgment for the following passages quoted in the text
'Something is turning up' and other material on General von Tettau and Major Krafft (pages 13-14) are from
unpublished material furnished by the late Colonel Boeree.
'Seated in the planes like grim steel-jawed automatons' (page 16) and 'A shell rocked us' (page 20) are from
Carter, *Those Devils in Baggy Pants*.
'The apprehension and concern of the veterans' (page 16) is from Gavin, *Airborne Warfare*.
'The North Sea . . . was like a millpond' (page 16) is from Hibbert, *The Battle of Arnhem*.
'I glanced ahead and below' (page 8) is from Urquhart, *Arnhem*. 'Cassidy, the green light is on' (page 19),
'The 20-minute warning sounded' (page 20), and 'When the green light came on' (page 22) are from combat
interview material in The National Archives, Washington, D.C.
'Once again the thrill of falling' (page 25), 'I don't know but it looks like the end of the war' (page 25) and
'We may be going one bridge too far' (page 30) are from Hibbert, *The Battle of Arnhem*.
'We ought to have a corps' (page 91) and 'to take charge of the military organization' (page 91) are from
Saunders, *The Red Beret* as is 'Hallo, formation leader' (page 92).
'Planes dropped out of formation' (page 103) is from Garland and Smyth, *Sicily and the Surrender of Italy*.
'If it had not been for the Allied airborne forces' (page 103) is from Gavin, *Airborne Warfare*.
'I do not believe in the airborne division' (page 105), 'The activation and training of airborne units' (page 105),
and 'Mass in vertical envelopments is sound' (page 119) are from Huston, *Airborne Operations*.
'Small quiet groups sit under the plane wings' (page 121) is from Rapport and Northwood, *Rendezvous with
Destiny*.
'A shadow of an army' (page 145) and 'My dear General' (page 153) are from MacDonald, *The Mighty Endeavour*.

Air Assault: The Development of Air Mobility John R Galvin (Hawthorn Books,
New York)
Sicily and the Surrender of Italy Lieutenant-Colonel Albert N Garland and
Howard M Smyth (Government Printing Office, Washington)
Airborne Warfare James M Gavin (Association of the US Army, Washington)
Those Devils in Baggy Pants Ross S Carter (Signet, New York)
The Battle of Arnhem Christopher Hibbert (Batsford, London)
Arnhem Major-General RE Urquhart (Cassell, London)
The Red Beret Hilary St George Saunders (Four Square Books, London)
Airborne Operations James Huston (unpublished: prepared for the Office of the
Chief of Military History, Department of the Army)
Rendezvous with Destiny: A History of the 101st Airborne Division Leonard
Rapport and Arthur Northwood Jr (101st Airborne Division Association,
Greenville)
The Mighty Endeavour CB Macdonald (Oxford University Press, New York)
The Brereton Diaries Lieutenant-General Lewis H Brereton (William Morrow,
New York)